Attack of the Customers

Why Critics Assault Brands Online and How To Avoid Becoming a Victim

By Paul Gillin

with Greg Gianforte

AttackOfTheCustomers.com

Limit of Liability/Disclaimer of Warranty: While the authors have used their best efforts in preparing this book, they make no representations or warranties with respect to the accuracy or completeness of its contents and specifically disclaim any implied warranties of merchantability or fitness for a particular purpose. The advice and strategies contained herein may not be suitable for your situation. Consult with a professional where appropriate. The authors shall not be liable for any loss of profit or any commercial damages, including but not limited to special, incidental, consequential or other damages. Do not read while operating heavy machinery. May cause agitation.

For questions about reprints, excerpts, republication or any other issues, send an e-mail to info@attackofthecustomers.com.

For Lillian and Blair

Contents

CHAPTER 8: MAINSTREAM MEDIA — ENABLER OR ENFORCER?

The wounded giant is still a powerful amplifier, but traditional media increasingly takes cues from the crowd.

CHAPTER 9: AN OUNCE OF PREVENTION

Active listening and influencer relations are your best strategies for staying out of trouble.

CHAPTER 10: HANDLING AN ATTACK

What to do if your organization becomes a target.

CHAPTER 11: THE ATTACK-RESISTANT ORGANIZATION

Eight rules for building a culture that loves its customers.

Introduction

This is a book we've both wanted to write for a long time, but for different reasons.

The Internet is radically reshaping channels of communication and giving voice to the voiceless. The sudden empowerment of billions of people to speak seamlessly to one another and to the institutions with which they interact will have long-term consequences that we can't even imagine. One thing is for sure, though: People are going to bitch and moan a whole lot more, and we think that's really interesting.

The Cluetrain Manifesto — the 1999 essay that foretold the disruptive power of social media — laid out the premise that markets are conversations. Conversations are inherently two-way, and organizations that refuse to engage in them will increasingly find their viability threatened. When people self-organize against institutions that have lost their trust, the impact can be swift and sweeping.

Nowhere was that more evident than in the Arab Spring uprisings of 2011. Dictators who had ruled their people with brutal efficiency for decades were brought down by demonstrations that were organized primarily over social networks. At the same time, the Occupy movement in the U.S. called attention to the growing disparity between rich and poor in a country struggling to crawl out of recession. Like Arab Spring, the Occupy movement was primarily built on Twitter hash tags and a bottom-up organizational approach that enabled protesters not only to move fluidly around Manhattan but to spread the movement to dozens of other cities.

The same factors that affect those kinds of political changes are also at work in business. Online attacks by customers, shareholders and activist groups are growing in number and in scope, and many businesses now invite attacks without even knowing it.

Because of Facebook.

Brands have flocked to the global campfire, drawn by the promise of cheap word-of-mouth promotion driven by legions of adoring fans, but many don't realize the Faustian bargain they're entering into. Social networks are all about engagement, and public conversations can invite critics as well as fans. Few companies are prepared for this unsettling reality. Critics have historically been ignored or dealt with in hushed private negotiations. Now they're not only griping in public, they're doing it on branded destinations set up by the very companies they complain about.

Businesses that have been a victim of customer attacks have mostly bumbled their way through a response. Many go silent, which makes them look evasive or clueless. Some have tried to censor critics by deleting their complaints, which is like throwing kerosene on a brushfire. Others block customers from speaking at all, which makes you wonder why they bother being on Facebook in the first place.

Altimeter Group has tracked a significant increase in social media crises over the last 10 years. From 2001 to 2006 – when blogs were about the only social media tools available – the average was less than two crises per year. From 2007 to 2011, it had jumped fourfold to nearly nine per year.[1] It's probably no coincidence that 2007 was the year Facebook broke out of the pack and Twitter went mainstream. Whether this growth is explained by an actual increase in customer attacks or by greater media attention is an open question. We believe it's a little of both. Customers have become more comfortable with the tools needed to organize a campaign, the population of social networks has exploded and the media have had to learn to do more with less.

While the overall number of major crises is still small, lesser skirmishes break out nearly every week. Brands are learning to manage them before they get out of hand, but the process has taken on the characteristics of a brushfire. Every time you think you have one outbreak under control, the smoke starts rising somewhere else.

While we were writing this book during the first half of 2012, new attacks were in the news nearly every week. Several of these stories are explored in more detail in the following pages:

- Lowe's, the home-improvement giant, suffered a crush of negative publicity over the backlash from its decision to pull advertising from a reality TV show featuring Muslim families. Supporters and critics descended upon the Lowe's Facebook page to debate the company's actions, often using racist and inflammatory terms. Lowe's eventually deleted the entire comment stream and issued an apology.

- Angry fans of the Swedish car company Saab took to the Facebook page of former Saab owner General Motors to vent their rage at the Swedish company's bankruptcy filing. For more than a week, GM's Facebook page was overrun by protesters charging that the U.S. automaker's ownership of Saab had ruined the company.

- Fans of the popular fun site 9gag.com swarmed the Nescafé Facebook page after the company failed to choose 9gag's operator, Janos Szolnoki, as the finalist in a contest to win $5,000. Szolnoki, who planned to use the money to help his disabled brother, got 47,000 likes for his entry, but he didn't make the final round. Supporters set up their own Facebook page, Occupy unfairNes-cafe, to rally their cause.

- Chiquita's decision to boycott oil extracted from oil sands in Canada aroused a protest from activists who said the company's practice of continuing to buy Arab oil was hypocritical. A protest site called ChiquitaConflict.com was set up. Because Chiquita doesn't enable people to post to its Facebook wall, critics set up Boycott Chiquita - Support Ethical Oil and amassed a following of more than 2,200 in a little more than a month.

- Adidas was forced to pull a line of sneakers from the market just days after introducing them after criticism erupted over the design of the shoes, which featured attached rubber shackles. Adidas said the design of the JS Roundhouse Mids was intended to be "whimsical," but that didn't satisfy critics that included the Rev. Jesse Jackson, who said he intended to call for a boycott in 50 markets if the shoes went on sale.

- ChapStick and Huggies were among the companies that withdrew controversial ad campaigns because of charges that they offended different constituencies. ChapStick's ad showed the rear end of a young woman searching the sofa cushions for her lip balm. It drew hundreds of comments on the Facebook page. Huggies was the target of a petition on Change.org demanding that the diaper maker revise its male-oriented campaign to depict fathers as competent caregivers.

- Progresso Soup's whimsical weight-loss ad campaign threatened to be undermined by complaints about the company's use of the controversial chemical bisphenol A (BPA) in its packaging. BPA has been linked to everything from infertility to cancer and cardiovascular disease. A petition on Change.org amassed more than 110,000 signatures and scores of angry comments accumulated on Progresso's Facebook page before the company issued a statement promising to investigate alternatives.

- Chick-fil-A unleashed a social media storm by stating that the company contributed to anti-gay groups. A backlash that started on Facebook spread to mainstream media and even national politics, where former Arkansas Governor Mike Huckabee championed a counter-demonstration to support the restaurant chain.

- Progressive Insurance was savaged in social and mainstream media over a blogger's allegations that the company represented a driver who caused an accident that killed his sister, who was a Progressive policyholder. Although Progressive's actions weren't unusual under the circumstances, the charges undermined its carefully cultivated image as a friendly company and drove customer perceptions to a four-year low.

We come at this topic from very different perspectives. Paul has long been fascinated by the inversion of influence that social media enables. When he was writing *The New Influencers* in 2006, he spoke to Vincent Ferrari, a 30-year-old New Yorker who had posted a hilarious recording of a frustrating conversation with a high-pressure America Online customer service rep on his blog and become a media celebrity in just six days. Ferrari's recording sparked major changes in AOL's customer service organization and probably contributed to the company's decision to exit the business of selling dial-up Internet service.

The idea that one person's experience could spark that kind of institutional change was mesmerizing, and the timeframe now seems downright pokey in the age of Twitter.

Greg is a serial entrepreneur who founded RightNow Technologies with the mission to rid the world of bad experiences and in the process helped nearly 2,000 large consumer brands make customer experience the centerpiece of their market differentiation. Their software, now under the Oracle umbrella, is still the market-leading solution for managing multi-channel interactions between large enterprises and their constituents. RightNow conducted major studies around the world for many years to document the growing importance of customer experience to loyalty and business results. While CEO of RightNow, Greg typically visited executives in over 200 client firms each year across many industries and has addressed thousands of customers on the importance of customer experience.

This book is about how to anticipate, prepare for and defend your organization against customer attacks, but more importantly it's an argument for building an organization that values critics as allies. When customers complain, it's because they care. Organizations that shut them down lose the benefit of feedback that can make them better companies. We live in a time of unprecedented competitive pressure and markets that brutalize companies that fail to continually innovate. Why would any company want to ignore advice from its most important constituents?

Companies that are widely considered to be leaders in social media actually encourage customers to air negative experiences so that they can deal with them quickly and retain them as customers. Walmart, which has had plenty of experience with criticism, uses a Facebook app from Get Satisfaction on a dedicated feedback page and a small team of employees to redirect complaints toward a satisfactory resolution. Much-admired companies such as Southwest

Airlines and Dell Computer not only don't censor critics, they thank them.

That's because they know a secret: When customer complain openly, "not only are we able to fix their problem 98% of the time, but 42% of the people we refer to as 'ranters' actually become 'ravers,'" says Richard Binhammer, who was one of the early architects of Dell Computer's social media strategy. "That doesn't mean just saying thank you. It's about actively going from being a demoter to a promoter."

For many years businesses have had the luxury of managing customer dissatisfaction on the assumption that it was difficult and expensive for people to share experiences. Magazines such as *Consumer Reports* built a franchise on aggregating consumer opinion, but today there are literally hundreds of websites that do the same thing at little or no cost.

We've heard many marketers express fear over these developments. Their companies have a cultural aversion to negativity, and they worry that a few vocal critics will unravel years of reputation building.

In fact, that almost never happens. People accept the fact that every company has some unhappy customers, and they don't expect perfection. The occasional malcontent can do very little damage if a company has good practices in place to address problems and an open approach to listening. When problems occur — and this is common to many case studies cited in this book — it's because one customer's experience strikes a chord with others who have the same problem or because a controversial business practice has been dramatized in some way.

In Chapter 3 we describe one of the most famous attacks in recent memory: Dave Carroll's "United Breaks Guitars" spoof video of the damage his Taylor guitar suffered at the hands of Chicago baggage handlers. Carroll's attack tapped into the deep-seated resentment that many frequent travelers feel about the impersonal nature of air travel and about the bureaucracy of many institutions that frustrates our attempts at resolution. We are all Dave Carrolls at some level.

Raising the Bar

As frustrating as online attacks can be, they ultimately make us all more honest and accountable. We believe they raise the bar for everyone. The days are long gone when automakers could force inferior vehicles down the throats of customers who had few alternatives or when fast food restaurants could deliver calorie-laden menus to people who couldn't afford anything else. Globalization has given us plentiful choice, and social media disrupts the big advertising budgets that used to keep a few wealthy brands on top. Companies can no longer spend their way out of lousy products and a poor customer experience. Innovation, quality and a commitment to customer service have become the most important success factors in markets that commoditize with amazing speed.

Attacks have taught even the biggest brands how to be humble. There was no better example of this than Domino's Pizza, which featured a series of critical customer tweets in an ad campaign that promoted the company's commitment to improving the quality of its product. We love the Domino's example because it shows how a company can turn negativity to its advantage. We wish more companies had the courage, humility and sense of humor to view criticism as an opportunity to do better.

Jenny Dervin, the corporate communications manager at JetBlue, tells the story of how crisis invigorated her company and made it one of the most admired airlines in America. JetBlue struggled with growing pains during its first six years, culminating in an incident on Valentine's Day 2007, when an ice storm forced several of its aircraft to idle for as long as nine hours on tarmacs throughout the Northeast. The culprit was a company policy that discouraged flight cancellations. That may have made good business sense, but it was lousy customer relations, and the firestorm of anger that the incident unleashed caused a "radical change in the company," Dervin says.

Three years later, communications staffers took advantage of a break in the spring leadership conference to send out a single tweet: "What would you say to JetBlue leadership in 140 characters or less? They're watching."

As executives returned to the conference room a cascade of live responses began to pour in over Twitterfall, a service that displays messages in a waterfall format. Executives "were glued to the screen," Dervin remembers. "It was a moment, a pure exchange of ideas between leadership and the people who are affected by those decisions."

Throughout the day, executives repeatedly cited comments from the Twitter stream for guidance in making decisions. The experience demonstrated that "it's not about office politics; it's about making customers happier," Dervin says. Two years later, the American Customer Satisfaction Index ranked JetBlue as number one in America in customer satisfaction.

Putting It All in Perspective

We've divided this book into two major sections. The first focuses on attacks: why they happen, who's behind them, how they spread with lightning speed and what companies can do to respond to them. We share many anecdotes and perspectives both on the attackers and their targets. We look at what motivates attacks, how they unfold and the interplay between social and mainstream media that can elevate them to national or even global prominence. We also spend some time on customer review sites, which are revolutionizing industries ranging from hospitality to healthcare.

The second part is about building an attack-resistant company. Much of this section is based upon Greg's experience building five successful companies over a 25-year period. In the course of steering Brightwork Development and RightNow Technologies to market leadership, he spent time with thousands of customers learning what makes their businesses successful. His passion for bootstrapping is rooted in a belief that great companies are built not on the backs of large venture capital investments but on a commitment to doing what's right for the customer. He spelled out some of his experiences in his 2008 book, *Eight to Great: Eight Steps to Delivering an Exceptional Customer Experience*. We have revised and updated those lessons to adapt them to this new age of the empowered customer.

— Paul Gillin and Greg Gianforte, November 2012

Chapter 1: When Customers Attack

In March 2010, Procter & Gamble announced the most significant technical advance in disposable diapers in a quarter century. The new Dry Max line featured an absorbent gel that improved diaper efficiency while cutting materials and costs by 20%. The thinner diapers addressed the number one complaint of diaper customers, which was bulk, while also reducing cost and environmental impact. The innovation was so impressive that former President Bill Clinton praised the diaper for reducing landfill waste.

However, Rosana Shah of Baton Rouge, La., was not impressed. Shah had noticed a change in the Pampers Cruisers she used to diaper her baby several months earlier. "The new design had less cotton pulp and was missing the dry weave liner," she wrote in an e-mail interview. "The back of the diaper was just thin, papery diaper cover, no absorption material whatsoever." Worse was that the child had become afflicted with diaper rash. "Every time I tried to change her diaper she would cringe and cry," Shah wrote. "All she could voice at the time was 'it hurts.'"

Shah believed P&G had substituted a cheaper Cruisers for its existing product and not told anyone about it. "I called Pampers and complained and was told this was the first they were hearing of these issues," she wrote. "When I asked if there was a change in design, they denied it at first."

In fact, Shah's suspicions were correct. P&G had actually begun shipping the new product in August 2008, more than 18 months before it was announced. The practice is called slipstreaming, and it's common in high-volume consumer packaged goods markets that manufacture products by the millions at facilities around the world.

1

"Figuratively, if you've got 500 diaper production lines, you convert the first line on day one and 500 days later you convert the 500th," explained Paul Fox, P&G's director of corporate communications. "During that time, you've got a mix of the old and new product on the market." New products typically aren't announced until the distribution pipeline is full, but by that time millions of people may already be using the new product.

That was the case with Pampers Dry Max. By the time of the early 2010 rollout, more than 2 billion unbranded Dry Max diapers had already been sold "without issue," Fox said. P&G had carefully monitored its customer support calls for evidence of customer dissatisfaction but had detected nothing out of the ordinary. The company typically logs two complaints for every 1 million diapers sold, and there was nothing to indicate that Dry Max had moved that needle.

Not that P&G expected big problems. The company was well aware that the entire Pampers franchise depended upon customer trust. "Not a grain of sand was left unturned" in Dry Max safety testing, Fox said. "A brand whose whole equity is based on babies' welfare isn't going to do anything that poses any form of risk to a baby."

So staffers were understandably concerned when a Facebook group appeared in late 2009 entitled "Pampers bring back the OLD CRUISERS/SWADDLERS."[1] The group was launched by Shah after her visits to the Pampers Facebook page and Pampers website convinced her that "many parents were also experiencing confusion." The group's initial demands were simple: Members wanted P&G to bring back the old diapers. But as membership grew, the site became a lightning rod for an assortment of other complaints and accusations.

Building on early charges that P&G had failed to adequately disclose changes in the product, members began complaining of leakage and flimsy construction. By spring the discussion was centered on complaints that Dry Max diapers caused diaper rash.

Members reported that children were developing blisters within hours of being diapered with Dry Max. References to "burn marks" emerged, followed by reports of "chemical burns." One mother of multiples reported that all four of her children suffered severe diaper rash. The culprit was clear: Dry Max diapers were inflicting agonizing pain on babies.

No one was actually citing any scientific evidence to support the claims, and a few voices noted that gap. However, some doctors told parents that the diapers were a possible culprit, and that was good enough to stoke the outrage.

In February 2010, a visitor began a campaign called "Flood the CPSC!" encouraging others to take their complaints to the Consumer Products Safety Commission. Three months later, a group of parents filed a class action lawsuit.

At P&G's Cincinnati headquarters staffers were alarmed and perplexed. Diaper rash is an unfortunately common occurrence that afflicts about one in four babies at any given time. The company dispensed advice to concerned parents about the topic through a variety of channels, pointing out that while a tight-fitting diaper may create the conditions for diaper rash, the problem was not caused by the diaper itself.

Staffers were convinced of Dry Max's superiority. The product had been heralded as a breakthrough by *Good Housekeeping* magazine and had already received several awards. How could consumers not see its benefits?

Many of the 11,000 members of the Facebook group didn't. They believed that the thinner diapers were simply a low-cost replacement for the product they had known and loved. They believed P&G was shoring up profits at the expense of their children's health.

Standoff

As complaints piled up, a conspiracy mentality took hold. Visitors were griping about everything from rude P&G customer service reps to price changes. A change in a store display at a local Walmart was evidence that P&G was undertaking a stealth recall. Journalists were requesting interviews, and by late spring the story had begun showing up on local TV stations.

By the time Fox arrived on the scene, the Dry Max protest was beginning to spin out of control. Jodi Allen, P&G's vice president of North America baby care, was taking a personal role in countering critics, posting comments on the Pampers website, recording videos and posting to discussion groups. However, the volume of complaints was piling up too fast for the P&G staff to handle.

Facebook at the peak of the Pampers Dry Max Attack

Fox is a 30-year media relations veteran with more than a decade at P&G and experience with the customer skirmishes that are a constant fact of life at such companies. Fox first urged the team to investigate all possible causes for the complaints. Was it possible that the manufacturing line was compromised or that product had been tampered with in the field? Satisfied that the answer was no, he focused the strategy around a few core principles:

- Get P&G off the defensive;

- Dispel rumors that P&G would reintroduce the discontinued products;

- Educate parents about diaper rash;

- Refocus the discussion on the welfare of the children.

The final point was particularly smart. P&G was engaged in a vicious circle of accusation that had transcended diaper rash and become a proxy for helpless consumers versus heartless corporations. By concentrating on child safety, P&G effectively allied itself with its critics. No one had ever suggested that child safety was not the overriding concern of all parties. Accused and accuser were effectively now on the same side. That was an important step.

Pampers staffers also had to be encouraged to resist the temptation to counter point criticism, particularly that which was nothing more than opinion. "Responding to inflammatory stories that have little basis in fact is a distraction," Fox said. "Engaging on that level can be the equivalent of throwing gasoline on the fire." Basically, when critics become convinced you can't do anything right, then you can't.

Instead, P&G focused on educating dispassionate opinion leaders who appeared genuinely interested in hearing both sides of the story. It brought two groups of "mom bloggers" to Cincinnati to meet with executives and scientists and address their questions. [2] It stepped up advertising about the benefits of Dry Max and posted videos by leading pediatricians about the causes and treatment of diaper rash. "If parents weren't seeking medical attention or treating the diaper rash, that was a big concern," Fox said. "Our focus was 'We are both concerned about the pain of diaper rash. Let's seek treatment.'"

The company began making a more focused effort to spend time explaining diaper rash to parents who called. It even sent representatives into the field to meet with particularly concerned parents. The company invited media to Baby Care Headquarters in Cincinnati to meet with developers and product managers. In contrast to the earlier defensiveness P&G had shown about the controversy, it was now displaying complete transparency.

Vindication

The turning point came in early September when the CPSC, which had agreed to investigate the case after receiving hundreds of letters, absolved Dry Max of any responsibility for diaper rash.[3] By fall, the volume of complaints had slowed to a trickle, and P&G was no longer discussing the incident. Shah's group is still on Facebook, but new posts appear weekly instead of hundreds per day.

Even absolution from the government watchdog hasn't convinced critics. Shah charges that P&G enjoys a cozy relationship with the CPSC that may have prompted the agency to downplay its findings. She also cited media reports that claimed portions of the agency's report are missing. A spokesman for the CPSC said the agency works with hundreds of companies on various standards committees, and the charges of collusion are baseless. "Just because we know people doesn't indicate any impropriety," he said.

Fox called the collusion allegation "an insult" and said the only information missing from the report is that which was mutually agreed to be proprietary, a statement the CPSC spokesman confirmed.

Lessons

Could P&G have handled the Pampers Dry Max case better? Probably. It had little choice but to slipstream the product into the market, but the company could have better prepared for a negative reaction. The Pampers team was so convinced of the product's superiority that they focused more on the positive splash it would make in the market than the possibility that some people might be alarmed by the visible changes.

P&G knows better than any company that people treat their personal care products like an old friend. Change can be unsettling, in the same way that an old friend showing up at a party with a nose job and a new wife might cause unease for everybody.

The incident was also a classic example of the suspicion with which many people regard large companies. As a member of P&G's Digital Advisory Board, Paul has worked with brand managers in many of the company's divisions and been impressed by their commitment to quality and customer satisfaction. However, few customers have that insight. Many people see a large corporation as a symbol of greed. An incident like this appears to validate that perception.

Critics accused P&G of opacity in its initial response to customer concerns. There were valid reasons why the company didn't tell critics that the diaper's design had been changed before the official announcement. There was no way to fill the supply channel with the new product without slipstreaming, and P&G wanted to wait until Dry Max was available everywhere to turn on the marketing spigot. Dribbling out details months before the formal launch would have undermined the formal rollout and created confusion that the company was not prepared to handle. Nevertheless, plausible explanation would have been better than denial. Once the conversation shifted from accusations to education, the tone changed dramatically. Pampers sales quickly recovered after a brief decline, and complaints fell back into normal range.

The Dry Max crisis came at a time when P&G was engineering a companywide shift toward customer engagement through social media. Fox said the experience was a critical teaching point. "You can't join a community at a time of crisis. You have to already be invested," he said. "Becoming a trusted voice requires an investment of time, people and money."

The experience was a lesson for Rosana Shah as well. "We found parents and caregivers from as far away as South Africa, Australia, England, France and Germany. Everyone was scratching their heads wondering if it was just them," she wrote. "We turned out to be 11,000 members who made the media, government bodies and P&G finally take notice."

Although some people might have called it a lynch mob.

Customers on the Move

The Dry Max story is just one of many recent examples of the ways in which customers empowered by cheap and free publishing tools use their digital soapboxes to take their cases directly to the market. Years of frustration with outsourced customer service centers, byzantine phone response systems and e-mail response forms that disappear into black holes have created a lot of pent-up resentment. The outpouring of opinion and storytelling that we now see is driven by the fact that there's a chance that somebody out there might listen.

A protest that used to require letter writing and stamps can now be lodged in a few seconds with a tweet. Online petition sites like Change.org make the process of organizing a protest trivial. If the cause fails to gain traction, little has been lost. A tweet or Facebook post can attract a faster and more satisfying response than a call to customer service. A 2012 survey of 2,000 adults in the U.K. conducted by Fishburn Hedges and Echo Research found that 65% believed social media to be a better way to communicate with companies than call centers.[4]

Many businesses are now so concerned about negative publicity that they respond more quickly to complaints posted in social media than to e-mail and telephone inquiries. This only encourages more aggrieved customers to go public.

Has the volume of customer complaints increased with the rise of social media or are protests simply getting more attention? The answer is a little of both. Consumers are getting bolder about leveraging their social networks for action. Online advocacy actions grew 17% between 2010 and 2011, according to a 2012 study by fundraising software maker Convio.

More than 70% of 142 global chief communications officers surveyed in early 2012 said their companies had experienced a reputation threat in the past two years.[5] A 2011 survey of 826 business decision-makers reported that 65% believe new media have made managing crises more difficult, and two-thirds believe new media have also significantly increased the potential cost of a crisis.[6] An August 2012 survey of social media risk managers by Altimeter Group found that 66% identified reputation or brand damage as either a critical or significant risk.[7]

The increase in reports of customer attacks is partially explained by the ubiquity of easy-to-use social media tools, but the decline of mainstream media is also a factor. Customer attacks make a compelling and easy news story. All the background material is right there online, and instigators are easy to reach and willing to talk. We discuss the changing dynamics of social and mainstream media in Chapter 8.

Protesters in Your Living Room

Critics of companies, government organizations and even nonprofits today enjoy unprecedented power to assemble and make their voices heard. In many cases, these protests take place on the public Facebook pages of the organizations they target. This presents a problem that brands have never faced before. They believe they have to be on Facebook, and the culture of the social network demands open conversation. When the conversation turns negative, however, brands find themselves in the awkward position of hosting a protest in their own living room.

"There's never been a better time to be a critic," says David-Michel Davies, Executive Director of the Webby Awards, which recognizes customer service excellence.

Compounding the challenge for marketers and brand owners is the speed with which aggrieved customers act in social channels. The immediacy of Twitter permits a gripe to be forwarded to a potential audience of literally millions in a few minutes. Traditional crisis communications assumes that an organization under attack has at least a few hours to evaluate a situation and respond. Today that window has been reduced to minutes.

"In our brave new world of one-click communication, a CEO can go to bed on top of the world and awake in the morning buried under the rubble of his company's formerly pristine reputation," wrote Peter Blackshaw in his 2008 book, *A Happy Customer Tells Three People, an Unhappy Customer Tells 3,000*. And Blackshaw's book was published before Twitter had become a global source of real-time news. Today, it's more likely the CEO would be awakened at 2 a.m.

The Information-Empowered Customer

With information racing around the globe in a matter of seconds, and with anyone able to publish to a global audience, customers now have unprecedented choice and access to information about the decisions they make. This is rewriting the rules of business at a pretty basic level.

Innovative new products are quickly knocked off by overseas copycats and sold through digital channels at a fraction of the price that the originator can charge. Customers research their purchasing decisions online, tapping into peer networks, review sites, consumer advocacy blogs and domain experts long before they even begin to interact with a seller. Almost no amount of marketing can counteract negative word-of-mouth.

"Most purchases are more highly researched than ever before simply because the consumer has more access to information than ever before," said Steve Goldbach, Leader of the North American Consumer Packaged Goods Practice at market intelligence firm Monitor.

Goldbach believes customers are so overwhelmed with choice these days — and have so little time — that many aren't even conscious of why they make the decisions they do. The once-predictable marketing funnel, which assumed that customers came into a vendor's orbit with little information and were guided toward a decision, has been flattened. Today, customers may arrive at a vendor's door having already thoroughly researched the purchase and made a decision. That's the good news. The bad news is they may never even consider a vendor because of a negative reference from a trusted source or even from someone they've never met.

The Customer Service Difference

With so many sources influencing a decision, and with so little time available, customer experience has become one of the few sources of differentiation. The most effective way to improve customer advocacy is to improve customer service. RightNow Technologies found that 55% of North American consumers recommend a company because of customer service, compared to 49% who base a recommendation on product and 42% on price.[8] What's more, 85% of consumers said they would be willing to pay a premium to ensure a superior customer experience, with 28% saying they would pay a premium of 20% or more.

Customer service is actually a more effective driver of loyalty than the coupons, rebates and affinity programs that many companies use. A 2012 survey of 427 U.S. consumers by ClickFox found that 33% said "providing exceptional 24/7 customer service" was the best way to build loyalty, compared to just 20% who cited rewards programs and 13% who chose offers and promotions.[9]

Yet customer service remains one of the most poorly funded and least valued functions at many companies. Why invest? Service has traditionally been a cost center, and costs are something to be contained. Many companies still reward service employees based upon the number of calls they field rather than the satisfaction of the callers. Customer service operations are frequently outsourced overseas or parceled out to individual contractors who serve multiple clients and have no authority to take extraordinary steps to ensure customer satisfaction.

As we were writing this book, Paul heard the following exchange at a local event. We don't know the speaker's name, so we'll call her Sally:

Sally: "It's a sucky job at sucky pay, but I need it."

Companion: "Really? What do you do?"

Sally: "Customer service for ------------- Student Loans."

We hate hearing anecdotes like that. We feel sorry for Sally, but also for her employer. Every day Sally drags in to work at a loan processor to field calls from customers. Many of the callers are probably anxious about their ability to make their loan payments in a lousy economy. If they're like most Americans, they also have a negative opinion of financial services companies in general.

Then they meet Sally, a customer service rep who hates her job, hates her employer and probably hates them, too. Sally has no interest in changing anyone's opinion of her employer. She also has no interest in satisfying the customer. If she's like most customer service reps, she's rewarded for the number of calls she handles, not the happiness of the customer.

Sally's employer probably doesn't even know about her bad attitude. In a down economy, many companies figure people are happy just to have a job. If customers of this loan processor need to take out another loan — or if they're asked by friends to recommend a company for that purpose — there's nothing about their interaction with Sally that will cause them to recommend this one. The human face of the company is a bitter, disenfranchised cynic.

The systems that companies have put in place to field customer calls are notoriously bad. How many times have you been stuck in a voice response system that wouldn't direct you to a resolution of your problem or enable you to speak to a human being? Or have you ever had the experience of being asked for your account information three times on the same phone call? These annoyances are the consequence of incompatible customer response systems that have been pieced together over the years and made worse by acquisitions, divestitures and the selection of point products that don't integrate with one another.

We make matters worse when we put people on the front lines who are not predisposed to serve the customer. Sally's attitude toward her job is probably not unusual. A lot of people see customer service as a thankless job or an unpleasant side of other work. This can be a self-fulfilling prophecy. People who have a negative self-image are the last ones to put in customer-facing roles.

Researchers at the University of Melbourne surveyed 432 employees at a retail chain and compared their stated commitment to customer service with a psychological profile of their own self-image. They found that people with positive affectivity (self-image) were more likely to respond positively to customer complaints than those with low affectivity. Basically, people with a positive attitude saw a complaint as an opportunity to improve rather than a criticism of their own abilities.[10]

Interestingly, the researchers also found that people who have low affectivity responded less negatively to complaints than people who fell somewhere in the middle. These are the Sallys of the world. Their morale can't get much worse, so they perform at a consistently low level but don't complain very much to their employer. What's more, neuroscientists have documented that listening to protracted complaining affects people's mood, making them negative and unable to think creatively about problem solving. "The brain works more like a muscle than we thought," says Trevor Blake, a serial entrepreneur and author of *Three Simple Steps: A Map to Success in Business and Life*. "So if you're pinned in a corner for too long listening to someone being negative, you're more likely to behave that way as well."[11]

Perhaps this is one reason why there are so many Sallys in customer service departments: They work at a "sucky job" but don't raise much of a fuss. The problem is that they also do nothing to raise customer perceptions of the organization.

In the chapters that follow we will examine the new landscape of customer relationships. We chose to focus this book on customer attacks because we believe that it's the most visible way in which these relationships have changed.

No one likes being criticized, but the silver lining of a customer attack is that it usually makes the victim a better and more resilient company. Some of today's most progressive organizations in the use of social media were also some of the earliest victims of customer activism. We'll share with you what we've learned about how to build attack-resistant companies and ultimately how to create the kind of customer-centric organizations that today's transparent markets demand. Let's begin with looking at how the battle unfolds.

Chapter 2: How Attacks Happen

American beef processors weren't prepared for an article in a digital news startup called The Daily to ignite a decade-old controversy that bankrupted one company, nearly drove a second out of business and caused a 25% plunge in ground beef sales, all in the course of four weeks.

The March 5, 2012 report quoted two former microbiologists at the Food Safety Inspection Service criticizing the U.S. Department of Agriculture's continued purchase of lean finely textured beef — more commonly known as "pink slime" — for use in school lunches. Pink slime is beef trimmings that are mechanically processed, treated with ammonium hydroxide gas and mixed with ground beef to add bulk at low cost. The article in The Daily referred to the substance as "soylent pink" and "not meat."[1]

The next day a food blogger named Bettina Siegel posted a petition on Change.org that demanded the USDA discontinue use of the additive.[2] ABC News followed with a report that 70% of ground beef sold in U.S. supermarkets contained the substance. It rebroadcast a year-old video of British chef Jamie Oliver demonstrating how ammonia is used as a processing agent in pink slime to kill bacteria.

From there, the pink slime crisis exploded, driven by bloggers, Twitter, anti-slime websites and mainstream media, which followed the controversy but did little to calm the hysteria. Google Trends documented a more than 100-fold increase in searches for "pink slime" in March compared to January. Social media monitoring service Crimson Hexagon documented 490 mentions of pink slime on March 5 and 8,429 five days later. Food bloggers massed while supermarket chains and restaurants frantically tried to distance themselves from the product.

It took the USDA three weeks to reassure the public that pink slime is safe, but by that point the industry's largest producer, Beef Products, Inc., had already suspended operations at three quarters of its plants and idled 650 people. Less than a week after the USDA statement, AFA Foods, one of the largest ground beef processors in the U.S., filed for Chapter 11 bankruptcy, blaming the public outcry over pink slime.[3]

The beef industry was completely unprepared for the crisis, even though controversy over the additive had simmered for a decade. Pink slime was certified as safe and nutritious by the U.S. Department of Agriculture, so few in the industry expected a controversy to erupt over a product that had long been in widespread use. A lengthy analysis in the trade publication *Meatingplace* summed up the conditions that created a tinderbox.

> *"In the midst of a deep economic downturn, fed by revelations of fraudulent mortgages and foreclosures by banks, chicanery at Freddie Mac and Fannie Mae, with memories of Enron, WorldCom, Bernie Madoff and other scams still crystal clear, consumers are loaded for corporate bear and have the means to make their anger heard. Add to that the meat industry's long-standing aversion to inviting the public to witness the nitty-gritty process of making sausage; thanks again to the Internet, which makes industrial transparency not only possible but expected, and consumers think the meat companies are hiding something."[4]*

In short, the industry's aversion to talking about its processes, combined with a pejorative euphemism and repulsive images created a groundswell of panic. In the aftermath, even many critics said the crisis was driven by misinformation and hysteria made worse by government delay.

The beef industry could have been better prepared, though. Food companies know that contamination is a constant risk, and the public reaction to pink slime wasn't all that different from a reaction to an outbreak of salmonella or E. coli. In fact, pink slime was a much smaller problem because nobody got sick. Why didn't anyone see this coming?

Probably because the crisis plan that has served the industry well in past cases of contamination wasn't prepared for hysteria that had so little basis in fact. Mainstream media coverage of the incident focused far less on the beef than on the frenzy in social channels. The public reaction was bigger news than the health issues. This is one reality of the new media landscape: Truth is less important than people's perception of the truth.

The case also dramatized another new reality: News events are no longer the only driver. An influential person or group may create a crisis over an issue that no one has even thought about for years.

Storm over Slings

Such was the case with Motrin Moms. This 2008 firestorm that made international headlines began with a couple of West Coast bloggers who didn't like a video that had been on the Web for weeks. Jessica Gottlieb didn't start out to embarrass Johnson & Johnson (J&J). She just thought the $65 billion pharmaceutical giant's tongue-in-cheek advertising campaign about the orthopedic risks of wearing a baby sling was in poor taste.

The Los Angeles mother of two has no formal journalism background, but she's a good writer. Blogging was a natural outlet for her passion for the environment and sustainability.

"Since 1997 my only lifeline was my DSL," she said of her Internet service. In the old days she might have been called a stay-at-home mom. But today's stay-at-home moms can have nearly as much clout as the *Los Angeles Times*. There are 3.9 million women bloggers with children under 18 in the U.S. alone, eMarketer estimates.[5] Top mom bloggers count their daily visitors in the tens of thousands.

It was November 2008, and Gottlieb was sharing her opinion with a lot of people. Her writing talent led to assignments from websites like Green Options and the National Lampoon. She embraced Twitter in its early days, and by the fall of 2008 she had built a network of 1,000 followers. She also met scores of other mom bloggers through her prolific writing.

One of them is a Colorado photographer named Barb Lattin.[6] On Nov. 15, 2008, Lattin posted an entry on her blog about a video ad she had seen for the Motrin pain reliever made by J&J. The animated spot was a lighthearted play on the growing popularity of baby-wearing. A voiceover by a 20-something-sounding woman asserted that the practice had some unexpected consequences. "They say that babies carried close to the bod cry less than others. But what about me?" the narrator asked. "Do moms that wear their babies cry more than those that don't? I sure do."

The ad had actually been online for six weeks before Lattin noted it. Gottlieb saw Lattin's post and took a look at the ad. She didn't think it was funny at all, particularly since this was the first International Babywearing Week. She posted a short article on a website called Eco Childs Play and linked to a post on the Green and Clean Mom site that questioned "what team of idiots decided that this would be a good message to send." She then posted a tweet challenging her followers to switch from Motrin to generic ibuprofen. Within a few hours, the #MotrinMoms hash tag was the number one search term on Twitter.[7]

Gottlieb knew using all the outlets at her disposal would collectively grow awareness of her cause. She also posted articles on the websites LA Moms and Silicon Valley Moms, as well as on her own blog, and linked them together. As the community of mom bloggers tweeted up the #MotrinMoms hash tag, the cause took on a life of its own. On Saturday night, about a day after the controversy began, Gottlieb chaperoned her daughter's slumber party, working on her laptop while watching the girls out of the corner of her eye. By that time Twitter traffic on #MotrinMoms was running at 300 comments per hour.

The next day, blogger Katja Presnal posted a YouTube video showing anti-Motrin posts juxtaposed with images of happy mothers carrying their babies.[8] By now, the media had taken notice and reporters were calling J&J officials — who were unaware that the protest was even happening — for response. Kathy Widmer, vice president of marketing at McNeil Consumer Health Care, the J&J division that makes Motrin, e-mailed apologies to several outraged mothers by Sunday evening, and the Motrin website was shut down at 9 p.m. It reopened the next day with a terse 102-word apology as media outlets, including *The New York Times*, *USA Today* and *The Wall Street Journal* reported the story.

"We have heard your concerns about the ad that was featured on our website," said Widmer's note. "We are parents ourselves, and we take feedback from moms very seriously." Marketing guru Seth Godin called Widmer's note a "carefully crafted non-statement of a committee," and he had a point. Simply using the first-person singular instead of the royal "we" would have made the message more genuine.

J&J has said little since then about the Motrin Moms incident. Perhaps even its own brand of pain reliever couldn't banish the headache that thousands of angry mothers had caused. Gottlieb said the only follow-up she ever heard from the company was when a senior executive approached her at a conference two years later and remarked, "We really blew that one, didn't we?"

Tempest in a Teacup?

Motrin Moms became an instant classic case study for the power and speed with which emotions can boil over on the real-time Internet. While it wasn't the first Internet attack, it combined multiple media in a way that no one had seen before. Blogger outrage was amplified by Twitter with unprecedented speed. The hash tag, which had been invented by Twitter users as a way of categorizing messages, enabled interested onlookers to filter and follow events as they developed. Reaching "trending" status was the equivalent of leading the evening news in the Twitter world. A video patched together in a few hours with low-cost editing tools added human drama. All of these moving parts came together without any central coordination or even clear leadership.

The speed impressed even an experienced blogger like Gottlieb. "I was amazed that my tiny corner of the Web was able to move people to take action," she said. "It drove home to me how much difference my words can make."

PR guru Peter Shankman was blunt in outlining the consequences for corporate communicators. "Say goodbye to focus groups; use Twitter," he wrote. "That both Motrin and their [sic] agency [weren't alerted earlier to the crisis] is pathetic. It's even more pathetic for their agency. ...Way to not do your job for your client."[9]

Yet for all the publicity Motrin Moms got, it's hard to argue that it was a full-blown attack. *Ad Age* put the impact in context, noting that the collective Internet storm "received less exposure than one 30-second spot on a cable news network" and accusing J&J of giving in "to a vocal flash mob that represents a tiny fraction of moms."

Lexalytics ran a sampling of tweets through its sentiment analysis engine and concluded that only about 58% were negative, which indicates that a significant minority of those who commented didn't have a problem with the ad. "If Motrin's brand managers were not just listening to the market, but accurately measuring it, too, they might not have been so quick to panic and pull the ad," wrote Lexalytics' Christine Sierra on the company blog.[10]

Even influential mom blogger Erin Kotecki Vest agreed that the reaction was out of proportion to the ad's offensiveness. "What happened this weekend went from smart, powerful activism to Palin-rally lynch mob," she wrote.

That was four years ago. Today we almost take the velocity of Motrin Moms for granted, and the hesitation that J&J exhibited in its response would be considered unacceptable.

No Time to Wait

The pink slime and Motrin Moms cases epitomize the conundrum that faces business communicators today. How do you know when an attack crosses the threshold from a few people venting to a full-blown crisis? And how do you know what response is appropriate when you haven't the luxury of time?

"Timing is a key element in any crisis management program," wrote Katie Paine in her 2011 book *Measure What Matters.* "While in the past, decisions and official statements may have waited until the deadline, with the advent of social media there is no deadline. …Where you used to have hours you now have minutes to articulate a response."[11]

Bad news spreads today with breathtaking speed, and our natural instincts can be our worst enemies. The human response is to end the confrontation quickly. It seems easiest to apologize and maybe offer some modest compensation, but that's rarely the wisest course. In fact, an apology that appears disingenuous or hasty can actually further inflame the attacker's indignation.

"Faced with the threat of possible attack, our natural inclinations are either to fight or to flee," wrote Janelle Barlow and Claus Møller in their 2008 bestseller, *A Complaint Is a Gift*. "Neither of these behaviors is appropriate in a business environment. …But they are natural responses that we suppress."[12] Hollywood reinforces this ineffective response by repeatedly depicting scenes in which a harried employee flies off the handle, insults the customer and walks off the job. Audiences love the drama, but it's a lousy lesson in customer service, the authors note.

One of J&J's mistakes in responding to Motrin Moms was to apologize and walk away. In the aftermath, even some of the bloggers who were involved in the incident commented that their goal was not to embarrass J&J but to engage in a conversation with the company. They wanted to help the pharmaceutical maker understand their point of view, but the company showed no interest in hearing them.

A more effective response would have been for J&J to explain that the ad was meant to be humorous, apologize for not anticipating the possible negative reaction and ask moms to join an advisory panel to review future messages. The company could have left its critics feeling good about effecting change instead of bewildered about why J&J shut down the discussion.

Paine notes that shoot-from-the-hip reactions are rarely a wise course. "You need data that comes from daily — or even hourly — monitoring of what is being said about you. Schedule delivery of these reports to allow plenty of time to craft and refine the key messages you need to be communicating...A well-managed crisis gets all the bad news over with and up front by aggressively dealing with the problem, and the volume drops precipitously after the first week."

The beef industry had plenty of data. Restaurant and supermarket chains were abandoning products containing pink slime in droves. The industry's problem was that it didn't know how to fight a trench war in social channels.

The Cattlemen's Beef Board and National Cattlemen's Beef Association maintain a website associated with its advertising campaign (BeefItsWhatsForDinner.com) that has an active companion Facebook page and a modest Twitter presence. However, neither was used to much effect when the pink slime crisis erupted. The Facebook page administrator posted a few responses to questions from visitors about the issue, but the strategy was purely defensive. The Twitter account never even mentioned pink slime.

The beef industry has no active blogger relations program, meaning that grassroots channels were all but cut off to it. Beef Products launched a "get the facts" website called BeefIsBeef.com, but there was no other organized industry opposition. Beef Products has no Facebook or Twitter following, so it was limited to counterattacking through mainstream media. It had one hand tied behind its back.

A more effective response would have been for the beef industry to leverage its large Facebook fan base to create a page devoted to debunking pink slime myths and to reinforce its beliefs with a swarm of statements from scientists and public health experts supporting the safety of the product. However, the *Meatingplace* article noted that the industry's traditional approach has been to shun publicity and keep its processes out of the public eye. That's perhaps understandable, but these days it's not very viable. Even companies whose processes aren't appetizing to watch need transparency strategies.

Most important, they need a plan that outlines response tactics to the most common attack scenarios. By knowing how attacks typically unfold, by clearly defining roles and time frames and by rehearsing the plan periodically, you can head off most crises. We outline steps you can take in Chapter 10. The worst course of action is no action at all.

Silence Amidst the Storm:
The Komen for the Cure Affair

Learn from the mistakes of the Susan G. Komen for the Cure debacle. In January 2012, news leaked that the respected breast cancer awareness organization had withdrawn funding for breast cancer screening programs for low-income women that were conducted by Planned Parenthood. Komen said the funding was canceled because of a new policy that prohibited grants to organizations that were under investigation. At the time, Planned Parenthood was the subject of a congressional inquiry over allegations that it used federal money to fund abortions. Komen said Planned Parenthood's funding wouldn't be restored as a consequence.

However, critics saw a deeper political motivation, particularly since Komen's newly hired senior vice president for public policy, Karen Handel, was an outspoken critic of abortion. Whatever the group's motivations may have been, a firestorm quickly erupted.

"Within minutes, both Facebook and Twitter were swamped with pro-Planned Parenthood, anti-Komen comments," wrote nonprofit marketing expert Kivi Leroux Miller on her blog.[13] "At one point last night, I did a quick count and found the ratio of anti-Komen's decision to pro-Komen's decision to be about 80 to 1 on Twitter."

Miller's 1,200-word analysis of the controversy was posted just 24 hours after the original story broke and updated several times over the next two days with commentary, videos, tweets, screen grabs from Facebook and quotes from mainstream media. Another prolific blogger, Dan York, posted his own 1,200-word assessment the day after Miller's, calling the controversy a "Colossal PR Train

Wreck."[14] Both posts contained dozens of links to other blow-by-blow accounts and analyses.

These were layered on top of the more than 8,000 comments posted on Komen's Facebook page. No one knows how many Twitter messages were logged, but the number was easily in the tens of thousands during the first two days. Three days after the crisis erupted, *The New York Times* called the organization's self-inflicted wounds "perhaps mortal."

"They have not helped themselves at all with their complete lack of preparedness and inability to communicate effectively," said Shel Holtz, cohost of the For Immediate Release podcast. "They may have destroyed their brand permanently."[15]

That all happened in less than five days.

The damage to Komen would have been far smaller had the organization said anything, but it remained resolutely silent as criticism mounted. When Komen finally did release a statement, it merely reiterated its position in language that read like a corporate press release. The group never addressed the hundreds of critical comments on its Facebook page. Handel resigned a few days later, but she went out with a bang, telling The Daily Beast's Abigail Pesta, "Planned Parenthood is a gigantic bully, using Komen as its own personal punching bag."[16]

Komen's reaction to a social media crisis was a textbook example of nearly everything an organization under attack *shouldn't* do:

- Stay silent, even after the story has jumped to mainstream media;

- Issue press releases instead of putting forth human spokespeople;

- Show disregard for the emotions underlying critical outrage;

- Restate past positions without elaboration or promise of reconsideration;

- Attack the attackers;

- Blame others for not being able to keep a secret.

Only time will tell whether the crisis permanently damaged Susan G. Komen for the Cure's reputation. However, the overhang was apparent months later when the organization's annual Global Race for the Cure drew about 25,000 people to Washington, about one-third fewer than the previous year. Similar declines were reported in Seattle, Tucson, and Winston-Salem, N.C.[17]

Time pressure places new demands on business professionals and communicators to anticipate problems rather than simply react to them. "You don't have time to bring in the lawyers," says Holtz, a veteran corporate communications and crisis management professional. "The lawyers, HR and communications people need to have talked in advance so they know what can cause problems. The approval process has to be proactive rather than reactive."

"No response can be quick enough, and the ability to act rapidly requires the constant, proactive monitoring of social media — on weekends, too," wrote *McKinsey Quarterly*.[18]

J&J could have mitigated the impact of Motrin Moms by having a standing panel of customers to review all its marketing messages for appropriateness. This would have at least given the company some deniability. J&J also missed out on an opportunity to find a silver lining in the crisis. Instead of issuing a curt apology and going silent, it could have reached out to the critics who led the attack and invited them to become part of an advisory council. It also could have used the incident to justify increased investment in social platforms that it could apply in the event of another attack.

Yet to this day J&J has done neither. Its sole Twitter presence is @MotrinMoms, an account it created during the 2008 crisis in a futile attempt to engage with critics. Abandoned in 2010, it's a pathetic memorial to a company that could have learned from a crisis but didn't. Its Facebook presence is similarly ghostlike.

J&J evidently didn't learn much from the Motrin Moms crisis. It's too early to assess whether the beef industry has learned from pink slime. What's clear is that having the channels in place to communicate as broadly as possible to all the influencers is increasingly a cost of doing business.

Chapter 3: Studies in Social Media Crisis

Let's look at several other examples of how social media-driven attacks unfolded in real-world situations. These include a case study that documented the spread of an attack from a single e-mail to national awareness, how a savvy communicator's lickety-split response and personal connections stopped an evolving attack in its tracks and even how Walgreens anticipated an attack months before it occurred. And there's more.

How an Attack Spreads:
The Aviva Complaint

A customer attack on Aviva, a U.K.-based insurance company, shows how all the elements of new media can work together to create a perfect storm. One customer with an agenda and knowledge of the social channels available to him can cause disruption that reaches the highest levels of a company and embarrassment that lasts for years.

Aviva customer Karl Harvard was exasperated with the insurer's customer service systems after his attempts to set up a debit account for his premiums subjected him to a gauntlet of ineffective automated voice response systems, long hold times and abrupt hang-ups. On July 17, 2009, he sent a critical but humorous letter to the company's CEO documenting his frustration.

Harvard was no ordinary customer, though. An advertising agency executive with many years of online experience, he also took his case to the social Web. He posted a copy of his letter on SlideShare and an account on his personal blog, A Grapefruit Matter.[1] He also shared his story and a link to the document on SlideShare with three popular U.K. consumer advocacy sites.

Somatica, a British reputation management firm, tracked awareness of Harvard's complaint as it spread through social channels.[2] Somatica noted that viral awareness campaigns typically need a trigger, and in this case it was, ironically, Aviva itself.

Someone posted a link to Harvard's blog entry on Aviva's internal website on July 23, 2009. Traffic to A Grapefruit Matter exploded to more than 2,000 visits that day. Aviva employees were evidently interested in the customer's experience because several contributed encouraging comments to the blog.

Another trigger was the customer service rating site Plebble.com. It posted Harvard's complaint as "front page news," and visitors voted it the most popular item of the day. All of those factors combined to make Harvard's gripe the third most popular document on SlideShare for that week.

Then there was good old-fashioned e-mail. Because the PDF on SlideShare was downloadable, readers could easily attach it to e-mail and send it to their friends. This evidently happened, since 89% of the traffic to Harvard's blog was "direct," meaning that the source couldn't be identified (e-mail is a major driver of direct traffic). Website statistics showed that awareness was spreading throughout the U.K. At first, most visits to Harvard's blog came from the area of Aviva's main office in Norwich, but over a two-week period traffic was detected from 274 different networks across the U.K. and on three other continents.

Aviva wasn't sitting still. The company's director of sales and marketing called Harvard personally to apologize and resolve his problem. Harvard graciously posted a follow-up entry complimenting the company for its personal outreach. Plebble did the same. By this point, however, the search engines had kicked in, and the Plebble report was ranked number two for a search on "Aviva customer service." The SlideShare document and blog entry were ranked sixth and 11th respectively. The incident was also showing up on FriendFeed and Tweetmeme, which is a diary of popular Twitter topics.

One month after Harvard had posted his letter, measurable views had surpassed 10,000. There's no way to know how many other people read the document via e-mail. Three years later, Harvard's complaint was still the seventh Google result for "Aviva customer service," proving that what starts in search tends to stay in search.

Lessons Learned

Karl Harvard's story had all the elements of a classic viral customer attack:

- The experience was, in Harvard's words, "an absolute nightmare." So many systems failed in the process of handling a rather simple customer service request that the story itself makes for compelling reading.

- Harvard's razor wit made his letter laugh-out-loud funny in places. Humor is a huge driver of viral awareness.

- Anyone can sympathize with his plight. We've all been there.

- Customer advocacy sites are major amplifiers of an individual's bad experience. A link from Plebble was all the search engines needed to quickly drive the story up the rankings.

- SlideShare's search visibility, download and embed capabilities made it easy for others to find and spread the story through their social channels.

- Aviva acted commendably in moving quickly to resolve the complaint, and both Harvard and Plebble were courteous in documenting the company's efforts. However, the genie was out of the bottle at that point.

- Harvard complained to a customer service rep about the way he was being treated before writing the letter, but she was either unable or unwilling to solve his problem. Most customers try to resolve issues with a company before going public. However, few customer service reps are taught to recognize these warning signs.

- Inbound links to Harvard's blog will keep the story in the public eye for some time. Once a complaint goes viral, search engines can give it considerable longevity. Prevention is the best treatment.

Grace Under Pressure: Ford's Ranger Station

The morning of Dec. 10, 2008, started out like any other for Scott Monty. The head of social media at Ford Motor Co. arose at 5:30 a.m. and checked Twitter to see if anything had come up overnight that merited his attention. As the simplest and most readily available social media tool, Twitter is an early warning system of developing storms.

This morning there was a problem lurking. A tweet sent at 1:30 a.m. warned "This is about as bad as PR gets for Ford right now!" and included a link to a site where a dispute that had started the previous afternoon was being documented in detail. The center of the firestorm was The Ranger Station, a popular site for off-road truck enthusiasts. The owner of the site, Jim Oakes, had received a letter from Ford the previous day demanding that he surrender the website's domain name and pay $5,000 restitution.

Oakes panicked. He didn't have the money, and he didn't want to surrender a community that he had built brick by brick for a decade. So he did what a lot of people do these days: He posted his dilemma to The Ranger Station community and asked for help.

Within minutes, members were responding with messages of support for Oakes and cries of outrage at the evil corporation that was attempting to destroy one of its biggest fans. Other enthusiast sites picked up on the discussion and ignited fires of their own. A lot of people were very angry, and Ford looked very bad. More than 1,000 angry e-mails poured into Ford's customer support mailbox in the first few hours.

Monty knew he had to respond fast, even though he had few facts to go on. At 7:29 a.m. he posted the first of what would be nearly

140 Twitter messages that day. It simply said that he was looking into the matter. He also placed a call to Ford's Associate General Counsel to find out the company's side of the story.

Scott Monty

It turned out Ford had a legitimate gripe. The Ranger Station has been selling decals bearing the Ford logo, a clear violation of the company's trademarks. The cease-and-desist letter was an attempt to get Jim Oakes to stop the practice, and the $5,000 fine was simply a scare tactic. But the message from the lawyers, cloaked in legalese, had gone too far.

Monty worked with the lawyers to craft a formal response, but he knew that simply posting a legal document on a website wouldn't calm the growing resentment. In fact, a statement framed in frigid legalese might make things worse. He picked up the phone and called Jim Oakes, whom he later described as "a really, really nice guy." Oakes said he was unaware that he was violating any laws by selling the Ford-branded merchandise and would immediately stop the practice. Monty explained in plain English what the lawyers wanted and the two parted on good terms.

Monty knew what would happen next. Oakes posted an account of the phone call on The Ranger Station. In social media, nothing stays confidential for long. During the call with Oakes, Monty made every attempt to be gracious and transparent. He knew that was the right thing to do, but also that the victim's account of the call would be his best air cover.

That's exactly what happened. As the negative comments continued to swirl on Twitter and elsewhere, Monty posted links to Oakes' account of the conversation. He also linked to Ford's official statement and reassured critics that the issue had been resolved. Finally, he tapped into his personal Twitter network of 7,600 followers (it's now nearly 10 times that large) to ask them to re-tweet the news that the issue had been resolved. Many of them did so. At

31

2:30 the next morning, Monty posted his final tweet of the day and went to bed. The great Ford Ranger Fire of 2008 had been extinguished.[3]

Lessons from The Ranger Station

Monty is the type of corporate communicator any company would be lucky to have. Nearly everyone who is active in the social media ecosystem in the U.S. either knows him or knows of him. A former advertising agency account executive, writer and prolific blogger, he took on the newly created social media manager position at Ford in 2008, just as the company was clamoring back from a brush with bankruptcy a year earlier.

Near-death experiences can be liberating for a business because they give it latitude to break the rules. Alan Mulally joined Ford from Boeing in the fall of 2006 with a charter to reinvent the company around innovative new vehicles and intense customer interaction. He wanted to use the new breed of social media tools, and there were few people better versed in them than Monty.

Monty had the credibility and relationships to personalize the Ford story. Plus he had a reputation as a heckuva nice guy. "You would think that with all this prominence and access to powerful people, Monty might become as inaccessible as prominent executives so often become, but he has not," wrote author and social media thought leader Shel Israel on Forbes. "Despite the fact that Monty…has earned a seat at a big-time decision maker's table, he has, by all accounts, remained transparent, accessible, self-effacing and at times even playful."

Monty had been at Ford only a few months when The Ranger Station crisis erupted, but his response aligned perfectly with the emerging culture of social media. Here are some critical assumptions he made:

- **Everything is documented and shared**. Media relations professionals have long played a game with professional journalists over terms such as "off the record," "not for attribution" and "on background." There's an understanding that reporters will withhold certain information or keep the source anonymous in the name of maintaining a good relationship with a PR person. Those rules don't apply in social media. Indignant off-road enthusiasts don't know the rules and aren't interested in playing by them. Monty knew that everything he said would be transcribed, copied and posted in public. That meant courtesy and transparency were essential. He also knew that being a nice guy would work to his advantage.

- **Act quickly, but be honest about what you *don't* know**. As soon as Monty understood what was going down with The Ranger Station he posted a tweet informing people that he was looking into the situation. That's all he had to do. As details emerged, he disclosed them, even sharing personal opinions at times. "Getting our legal team's perspective and trying to stop a PR nightmare," he tweeted at one point that morning. The message was that Ford was taking the issue seriously and people should hold off on amplifying the problem because there was urgency about finding a solution. The "PR nightmare" reference was also a subtle message that Monty himself was under fire and to please give him a break while he did his job.

- **Correct inaccuracies**. It was neither practical nor effective to respond to every opinion that was being tweeted about the crisis, but Monty knew how quickly misinformation spreads online. He focused many of his tweeted comments on correcting mistakes so they wouldn't spread and ignite other brushfires. He also knew who the influencers were. Several of his tweets were directed to people whom he knew had the credibility within the community to reach others.

- **Humanize the interaction**. Monty knew that simply posting a corporate statement and walking away — as Johnson & Johnson had done with Motrin Moms less than two months earlier — would only make matters worse. Ford already looked like the big, bad corporate leviathan, so his goal was to make this a conversation with a human, not a brand.

33

- **Ask your network to help**. Once Monty had gotten to the bottom of the situation, he didn't hesitate to enlist his friends to help spread the message. "Here is Ford's official response to the fansite cease & desist debacle http://is.gd/b3qd #ford Please retweet," he wrote at 4:56 p.m. Twenty-five followers responded, amplifying the message to their networks.

Monty had spent years cultivating his personal credibility and social connections. Those paid off in The Ranger Station crisis because people who could have blown the controversy out of proportion saw that Scott Monty was on the case and gave him the benefit of the doubt. The same dynamic applies in traditional media, which is why experienced and connected PR professionals are so valuable. Reporters will give them a break because they know the pros can be trusted.

Monty also demonstrated the value of the human touch in the single most important step he took that day: calling the owner of the website. Once he and Oakes had connected on a personal level, Oakes became his most valuable resource. In this day of constant asynchronous communications, we sometimes forget the value of the human voice. Ford's lawyers could have benefited from that knowledge.

The Ranger Station crisis was resolved quickly and amicably in part because Monty understood the importance of speed, but also because he knew the value of relationships. "Whatever The Ranger Station crisis cost Ford in Monty's time and the time of other employees... I will guarantee it was a pittance compared to what the crisis would have cost had it grown," wrote Charlene Li in her book, *Open Leadership*.[4]

Anticipation: Walgreens Goes on the Offensive

Sometimes you can see an attack coming, and when you have that luxury, leverage all the tools at your disposal.

The giant pharmacy chain Walgreens chose to go on the offensive when a dispute with a business partner threatened to turn into a public relations mess. In 2011, Walgreens and pharmacy benefit management organization Express Scripts got into an ugly dispute over contract renewal terms. Unable to agree, the companies let their existing contract expire at the end of the year, leaving tens of thousands of Walgreens customers with the choice of shifting to a Walgreens benefit program or finding a new pharmacy (the two companies later reconciled).

Walgreens knew it had a potential crisis on its hands. Competitors jumped on the opportunity to woo customers away from the country's largest pharmacy chain, and Express Scripts was spinning the story as a money-grab by Walgreens. With more than 10,000 mentions of the Walgreens brand popping up in social media each day, Walgreens knew a conventional media strategy wasn't enough.

The retailer opted for a multipronged proactive strategy using a combination of paid and earned media. It knew that its strongest assets were devoted customers, and it mobilized to get them talking. With the luxury of some time to prepare for the news to break, Walgreens was able to secure the #ILoveWalgreens promoted trend on Twitter to appear just a few days after the Express Scripts contract expired.

"It's difficult to find something that will allow you to move as quickly as you can with social, to allow the information to spread as quickly and to be able to reach the right people," said Adam Kmiec, director of social media for Walgreens, in an interview on the For Immediate Release podcast.

We'll see shortly how promoted trends backfired for McDonald's, but Walgreens was confident that most customers would respond positively. Staffers continue to seed Twitter throughout the day with promotions for the Walgreens alternative benefit program as well as offers of special introductory savings.

The drug store chain also launched a website called IChoose-Walgreens.com to promote its alternative plan and position Express Scripts as the villain for limiting customer choice. It also engaged Social Spark, an agency that facilitates sponsored blog posts, to engage with people who blog about topics like value shopping, beauty and healthcare to publish advertising messages.

Walgreens' tactics were controversial and drew significant criticism. "The chances that [paid social media] will convince customers to switch plans through scripted blogs and tweets are slim, and could even backfire among those who view it as inauthentic," wrote *Advertising Age*. An accompanying unscientific poll showed readers believed the programs would hurt Walgreens more than help it by a margin of about five to one.[5]

However, Walgreens' Kmiec called the campaign a success. Social media monitoring tools showed positive tweets using the #ILoveWalgreens outnumbered negative tweets by a factor of 10:1. Kmiec told the For Immediate Release podcast that sentiment analysis was overwhelmingly in Walgreens' favor. "You can't let your actions be guided by potential headlines," he said. "You need to be guided by insights."

As of this writing, Walgreens was still struggling to recover business lost from the breakup with Express Scripts, but its efforts to contain the public relations crisis are widely seen as a success.

What's in a Name? The FM Global Transposition Error

Sometimes there isn't a damn thing you can do but play defense. Insurance provider FM Global learned that when it was briefly caught up in a global feeding frenzy triggered by, of all things, a transposition error.

Johnston, R.I.-based FM Global is a 177-year-old multinational company that provides commercial property insurance and loss prevention services for more than one-third of the Fortune 1000. It is not related to MF Global, a global financial derivatives broker that failed spectacularly in 2011 amid accusations of financial mismanagement.

Who Owns the Relationship?

There was a risk to Ford in placing so much responsibility for communicating about The Ranger Station incident in the hands of one person: Scott Monty's personal network is an asset that he owns. As an employee of Ford, he was able to leverage his connections to benefit the company, but what happens if he leaves Ford?

This issue has acquired increased urgency with the widespread adoption of social media for public relations, and it's one of the most common questions we hear from audiences. There's no single right answer to who should "own" a company's presence on Twitter, which supports both personal and branded accounts. Ford could have insisted that Monty communicate under the corporate brand, but it would have lost the benefit of his large personal network, as well as the human touch that was so important. On the other hand, Ford would have had complete control of the message and ownership of its follower base.

As of this writing, Monty has more than 82,000 Twitter followers compared to about 160,000 for the Ford corporate account. Some of Monty's large following is undoubtedly a side benefit of his prominent position at Ford, but there's no way to tell who those people are or what claim Ford might have to them.

Companies are increasingly encouraging employees to tweet about company business under their own handles with the goal of making business connections more personal. This is a great idea if you can pull it off. People relate a lot better to other people than they do to brands. When a crisis erupts, you want faces talking, not logos.

Just be sure you don't confuse customers. You can use a hybrid approach that appends the corporate brand to an employee's Twitter handle (for example, @LionelAtDell) or annotate business-related tweets with a hash tag like your stock symbol. Regardless of what you do, encode the rules in a formal social media policy that employees sign.

You should never demand or coerce employees into using their personal social media accounts to promote company business. Twitter users, in particular, regard their followers almost as personal friends. Asking them to tweet business promotions from personal accounts is as bad as expecting them to sell insurance at a kid's birthday party.

Attribution is also an issue on LinkedIn, which prohibits branded communication except in an official company activity stream. In other words, if your employees participate in LinkedIn groups, they do so as individuals, not as representatives of the company. This is rarely a problem, but a policy should require that personal opinions be disclaimed or that messages promoting a company be labeled as such. Again, enforcing such a policy is nearly impossible, but having it in writing buys you some protection.

This issue is almost certain to be addressed by the courts. In late 2011, a technology review site called Phonedog.com sued a former contractor to recover a Twitter following he had established while under contract with the company. Noah Kravitz had built his 17,000-member following while tweeting under the handle of Phonedog_Noah. When he left the company, both parties agreed that he could keep the following as long as he continued to post occasional promotional messages under the renamed handle of @NoahKravitz.

The relationship soured, though, when Kravitz filed suit for back pay. Phonedog went after Kravitz' Twitter following, valuing it at $2.50 per month per user, or $340,000 over eight months (we think the valuation is nuts, but we're not lawyers). As of this writing, the case was still working its way through the legal system.[6]

Following MF Global's filing for bankruptcy in October, 2011, public relations staffers at the insurer began to notice that a few media outlets and social media commenters had inadvertently transposed the first two letters of the companies' names. FM Global would quickly seek to have the errors corrected. Even an

Albanian news website displayed the insurer's logo in an article about MF Global's bankruptcy. What the public relations team didn't expect was to have future mistakes eventually create national headlines.

That happened early in December 2011 when the U.S. House of Representatives Committee on Agriculture held hearings looking into the problems at MF Global. Committee Chairman Frank Lucas (R-Okla.) mistakenly referred to the target of the hearings as "FM Global" four times during a Dec. 8 session.

The error was amplified by other news media during live broadcasts of the Congressional hearing. "On the morning of the hearing, my e-mail box began flooding with alerts," said Jamie Pachomski, senior public relations consultant at FM Global. "As we started seeing incorrect references in the media, people on Twitter picked up on the mistakes."

With the allegations in the hearing room stoking public upset, some of the conversation on Twitter took an angry tone. One user even snapped a photo of an airport ad showcasing FM Global's Research Campus that read "We play with fire so our clients don't get burned." Ironically, the user commented, "Bad symbolism," not knowing the photo in the ad was of the insurer's fire technology laboratory.

"Will now be spending the rest of my day tweeting nasty things about @FMGlobal," tweeted another.

FM Global's PR team took to Twitter and other online sources to defuse the crisis. "I began pulling out the Twitter handles of people we needed to reach out to and drafted a very basic message pointing out that they might have unintentionally mis-referenced us," Pachomski said. With FM Global becoming one of the top trending topics on Twitter — a company first — staffers also targeted journalists at key media outlets such as *The Wall Street Journal*.

Staffers benefited from the fact that they were able to respond immediately. "We knew what needed to be done and just did it," said Steve Zenofsky, manager of public relations. The PR team also decided at the outset to respond with a human touch and humor instead of displaying frustration. "We didn't want to come across as a stodgy insurance company," Zenofsky recalled.

Pachomski's relaxed but urgent Twitter banter called the transposition error "not cool" and during an interview with the *Journal*, Zenofsky was quoted as joking that the company's only regret about trending on Twitter was "We didn't bump Alec Baldwin," the actor who at the time was experiencing a minor PR crisis of his own. The conversation quickly began to turn as people corrected their Twitter mistakes. Media figures such as Dow Jones' Erik Holm later documented the mix-up on the *Journal*'s website and in a video interview.[7] *Fortune*'s Dan Primack also wrote about the goof.[8]

In the end, the experience helped strengthen some key media relationships and reinforced FM Global's message of industry leadership and financial stability. It also tested the public relations staff's crisis readiness. "Just because you know what you should do in a crisis doesn't mean you'll be ready when it comes," Zenofsky said. "Will you execute and get the outcomes you desire?" And while this particular crisis has dissipated, the issue continues to be managed. "The good news is each error becomes an opportunity for FM Global to become better known for the right reasons," he added.

FM Global's example also shows the value of covering all your bases to ensure that search engines don't perpetuate an error for years. Of nearly 22,000 Google search results linking "MF Global" and "FM Global," 70% now refer to media relations efforts that set the record straight. When the insurer's name is accidentally paired with "bankruptcy," the top three Google results link to media coverage of the error. Staffers have been invited to present their case at numerous universities and professional conferences.

When Image and Actions Collide:
The Progressive Insurance Fiasco

In the introduction we called Facebook a Faustian bargain. Few cases better illustrate the potential for the social network to backfire on a brand than that of Progressive Insurance.

Progressive has always fancied itself to be different from other insurance companies, and the ad campaign it debuted in 2008 was certainly out of the ordinary. It introduced the incongruous concept of a spotless white insurance retail store staffed by a relentlessly cheerful, if somewhat creepy, customer service representative named Flo who would stop at nothing to make customers happy. Over the course of more than 50 ads, Flo developed a reputation for snappy one-liners and built a cult following.

Flo became Progressive's social media mascot. By the time a crisis erupted in August 2012, her Facebook page had earned 4.4 million likes, or about 80 times as many as Progressive's company page. She also had almost 18,000 Twitter followers. In an industry that struggles with a perception of banality, Flo was a rock star.

But Flo had no witty comeback for a New York actor named Matt Fisher. On Aug. 13, Fisher posted an entry on his Tumblr blog that accused Progressive of offering legal advice to the driver of a car that had killed his sister two years earlier in Maryland.[9] His sister was insured by Progressive.

Progressive's actions in the case actually weren't all that unusual. Maryland has unorthodox procedures for handling liability claims that often force parties into the courtroom to assess damages. If the court had found that Progressive's client had any responsibility for the accident, Progressive could have avoided paying as much as $75,000 in claims.

There's a nasty contradiction in the insurance business. Companies have a fiduciary obligation to shareholders to minimize costs, and sometimes that means taking a stand against their own policyholders. That's one reason you never hear insurance companies advertise the size of their payouts.

41

Fisher's post quickly went viral on Tumblr, where it was reposted more than 11,000 times.[10] It lit up the Twittersphere, hit *The Wall Street Journal* and *The New York Times* and became a full-fledged media nightmare for Progressive in a matter of days.

This was a problem for Flo. The cute, kitschy icon was now associated with an act of corporate ruthlessness that stood at a sharp right angle to everything she was supposed to represent. Flo went dark on Facebook and Twitter for 15 days while hundreds of vicious comments piled up.

Progressive didn't help matters by posting a robotic explanation of the case on its blog under a corporate byline.[11] More than 130 visitors contributed comments, most of them viciously critical. Progressive didn't respond to any of them.

Progressive quickly settled the case and Flo crept back onto Facebook and Twitter without mentioning the controversy. How long the critics will forgive and forget is another matter. YouGov, an international Internet-based brand reputation monitoring firm, said consumer perceptions of Progressive plummeted to a four-year low in the two weeks following the incident.

The lesson: Social media is a two-way street, and if you're going to build a brand there, you'd better be ready for rotten tomatoes as well as bouquets. It's great when people spread your happy talk to their friend networks, but if your behavior doesn't align with your image, those ambassadors can turn into assassins pretty quickly.

Doh! Avoiding (or Profiting From) Self-Inflicted Injury

The most preventable form of attack is the self-inflicted injury. That's when a company or organization inadvertently lays the groundwork for a problem by creating a platform that invites hostility.

A recent example was the McDonald's #McDStories campaign, which had a brutally short run on Twitter in January 2012. The campaign was conceived to promote the burger chain's commitment to freshness by spotlighting its suppliers. A series of tweets sent Twitter users to promotional videos and case studies about family farms and fresh produce. On the afternoon of Jan. 18, a McDonald's marketer introduced the #McDStories hash tag as a promoted trend. Whoops.

Promoted trends are sponsored hash tags, and they are a popular advertising option on Twitter. The social network sells one promoted trend slot each day, and it guarantees that the hash tags buyers choose will appear at the top of the popular "trending topics" list. Promoted trends are instant Twitter visibility. The idea is to jumpstart conversation on a topic, if for no other reason than to satisfy people's curiosity about why the topic is trending.

Critics immediately took advantage of the #McDStories invitation to recount some of the most repulsive experiences they had ever had at McDonald's restaurants, as well as to trash fast food restaurants in general.

"Ordered a McDouble, something in the damn thing chips my molar," wrote one tweeter with the non-endearing handle "PuppyPuncher."

"Hospitalized for food poisoning after eating McDonald's in 1989," wrote Alice_2112, who clearly has a long memory. There were many other tweets like those.

"Within an hour, we saw that [the new hash tag] wasn't going as planned. ... It was negative enough that we set about a change of course," McDonald's' social media director Rick Wion told paidContent.org.[12]

McDonald's immediately stopped using the #McDStories hash tag in its own tweets, but the horse was out of the barn by that time. Months later, #McDStories was still being used to bash the company. It may still be around years from now.

Self-inflicted injury can also have a silver lining. That was the case with the country of Sweden, which launched a tourism campaign in

43

late 2011 that gave individual citizens control of the @Sweden Twitter account for a week. The promotion was intended to introduce people to the diversity of Sweden's population, and the sponsor placed few restrictions on what the temporary account-holders could say. The guest tweeters were nominated by peers and evaluated by a three-person panel. They ranged in age from 18 to 60, and their topics covered the gamut from food to politics to sex.

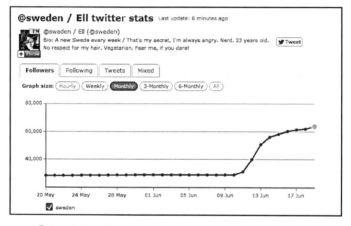

@Sweden's follower count more than doubled during a crisis

In June 2012, however, the experiment took a controversial turn when 27-year-old Sonja Abrahamsson posted several remarks about Jews that many people found objectionable. "In nazi German [*sic*] they even had to sew stars on their sleeves. If they didn't, they could never now [*sic*] who was a jew and who was not a jew [*sic*]," she wrote on June 12.

Media coverage was swift and mostly harsh. "Sweden's Twitter experiment goes off the rails," headlined *The Sydney Morning Herald*. "Sweden Twitter campaign marred by 'Jew' comments," remarked the BBC. "Swedish tourism Twitter initiative backfires," wrote the *Telegraph*.

Abrahamsson issued a half-hearted apology, but the government nevertheless allowed her to finish out her one-week term and said it had no plans to end the campaign. For good reason. The @Sweden follower count had more than doubled in one week (see image on opposite page). The website traffic-tracking service Alexa documented a tenfold jump in daily reach for the promotional CuratorsOfSweden.com tourism site. "Mathematically, @Sweden Is a Rip-Roaring Success," wrote *The Atlantic*'s Wire blog, which was one of the few to find the silver lining.

@Sweden was a classic case of Oscar Wilde's observation that "the only thing worse than being talked about is not being talked about." While the campaign had delivered steady growth to @Sweden's Twitter following, progress had been slow. Controversy took it to another level. The fact is a whole lot more people were talking about Sweden on June 13 than on June 11, and a few of them were probably taking a fresh look at the country as a vacation destination, judging by the spike in traffic to the sponsoring website. The controversy created a bounty of awareness, which was the whole idea.

talk is talk

Chapter 4: Why Customers Attack

"The beauty of the digital age is you don't have to take it anymore. You're no longer just screaming into the dark."

— Bob Garfield[1]

Throughout this book we will share stories of customer attacks catalyzed by everything from a $5 surcharge to global warming. What common threads run through these widely divergent stories?

We think there are several. In nearly every customer attack we've studied, the aggressors believe they were treated unfairly or that the company or its employees did something that offended them. In most cases, they also found that the accepted channels of response were either closed to them or had failed. And, in nearly every instance, the instigators either believed they spoke for a larger group or discovered that fact after the attack gained a groundswell of interest.

The most common cause of customer dissatisfaction is lack of respect, according to Guy Winch, author of *The Squeaky Wheel: Complaining the Right Way to Get Results, Improve Your Relationships and Enhance Self-Esteem*. Customers want the people and organizations they do business with to show respect for their time, dignity and intelligence. Yet businesses routinely sacrifice customer satisfaction for efficiency or cost control.

Consider the byzantine automated call response systems we've all encountered that force callers to navigate multiple menus when all they want to do is speak to a person. We key in account codes and Social Security numbers in response to a robotic voice only to be transferred to a human who asks us to repeat the information. It's no surprise that sites like GetHuman.com have sprung up to help people bypass this annoyance.

"Few of us enjoy being patronized or manipulated," Winch wrote in *Psychology Today.* "Keeping us on hold for thirty minutes while we're told how much the company values our time, having an automated message that sounds like Judy [*sic*] Dench when the person answering the phone sounds like Judy Tenuta, forcing representatives with thick foreign accents to pretend to have fake American names and hoping to buy our loyalty with free pens, useless knick-knacks and logoed lollipops, does not convey that a company respects our intelligence. Just treat us like adults."[2]

Numerous studies have documented the importance of fairness in good customer relationships. Few people complain because they want compensation. In fact, excessive givebacks can embarrass people and actually make them angrier. All they usually want is to get the problem fixed. And maybe an apology.

A 2006 study of complaint handling in hospitals found that nearly 80% of the complainants said their goal was to prevent the incident from happening again. Only 7% wanted financial compensation. Remarkably, many more complainants wanted an explanation (65%) than an apology (41%). The researchers concluded that the desire to fix things was born "not out of pure altruism, but in order to restore their sense of justice."[3]

Are people really that interested in doing what's right? It appears so. Perhaps that's because doing the right thing is the easiest way to get along with everybody else. Think about how we conduct our everyday lives. We willingly take our place at the end of a long line even though we might be able to talk ourselves into a better position. We often let drivers turn across our lane, even though we have the right-of-way, because it's the nice thing to do. When we see someone speeding past a cop sitting by the side of the road, we're angrier at the cop than we are at the speeder. Our sense of fairness has been offended.

The best way to mend a broken sense of fairness isn't necessarily to make the situation right for the angry customer but to explain how the incident happened and why it won't happen again. However, customer-facing employees are rarely rewarded for patience and listening. They're trained to resolve problems as quickly as possible. The most important part of complaint resolution is shoved aside because it's considered inefficient. What a shame.

Keeping Your Cool

In *A Complaint Is a Gift,* Janelle Barlow and Claus Møller make the case that angry customers seek explanation more than compensation. By showing sympathy for their position and a willingness to do better, we can deflect the vast majority of customer complaints. The authors cite a survey of 700 problem incidents in the airline, hotel and restaurant industries that found that fully one quarter of customers' positive memories actually began as problems. The willingness of company representatives to listen and understand made the difference.

Most people don't handle confrontation very well, however. Angry people lack perspective and so blame individuals for the failure of the system rather than the system itself. They want the person standing in front of them to accept responsibility and make things right. We've all felt this way. When the gate agent announces another two-hour delay or bumps us off our flight, we want to grab the person by the throat even though we know the fault isn't hers.

Human nature also isn't to accept complaints graciously. Our first reflex is to become defensive. We deny that the problem occurred, blame it on the customer or attribute it to a bad policy or procedure. So the gate agent throws her hands in the air and says, "There's nothing I can do," when a more effective response might be, "Yes, I know this stinks. Believe me; no one wants to get you to your destination faster than we do." Since few people are very good at listening in confrontational situations, their response usually makes matters worse.

Dissatisfaction often comes down to perspective, which people on opposite sides of a conflict rarely have. One study found that in a confrontation, employees tend to blame customer dissatisfaction on external factors and unrealistic customer expectations rather than on their own behavior. Customers, on the other hand, tend to blame the employee.[4] It's hard to reach consensus when the parties can't even agree on where the problem lies.

Only after their complaint has been heard and understood do people expect an apology, and many people don't even want that. Apologies do no good if they don't address the failure that caused the problem. Barlow and Møller note that an apology delivered too quickly can worsen the situation by looking like a brush-off.

Compensation isn't necessarily the answer, either. While upgrades and coupons can be useful tools when delivered with sincerity, they can also backfire. An upgrade presented with a scowl says, in effect, "Take this and get out of my face." People don't want their complaints trivialized. Barlow and Møller make the case that giving people more than they believe they deserve can actually embarrass them and make them angrier. There's that sense of fairness again.

The authors outline what they call an "Eight Step Gift Formula" to calm all but the most outraged customers:

1. Say "Thank you;"

2. Explain why you appreciate the feedback;

3. Apologize for the mistake;

4. Promise to do something about the problem immediately. Take responsibility;

5. Ask for necessary information;

6. Correct the mistake — promptly;

7. Check customer satisfaction;

8. Prevent future mistakes.[5]

The first item on the list appears to make no sense. Why would you thank someone who's making your life miserable? But the authors say this tactic is amazingly effective. A thank-you shows that the listener is receptive and that the organization is open to improvement. It's disarming; how can you stay angry at someone who has just expressed gratitude for your feedback? It makes the customer a partner instead of an adversary, and it sets the stage for the other seven steps in the process.

Items #4 through #6 are often problem areas. Customer-facing representatives may promise to take action, but the issue either falls through the cracks or gets lost in the bureaucracy. In Chapter 5, we share the experience musician Dave Carroll had with United Airlines that prompted him to create a satirical video that went viral to the airline's embarrassment. Carroll's frustration was with the failure of its grievance system more than about restitution. Any tools you use to address customer complaints, from pencil and paper to sophisticated CRM, should require resolution to be logged before the issue is closed. RightNow Technologies' 2011 Customer Experience Index Report found that 71% of consumers who have shared complaints about poor customer experience online believe their complaints were ignored. When you post on Facebook that you're looking into a problem, be prepared to provide regular status updates and a resolution. The Internet doesn't forget.

Another critical item on the list is #7. Few people on the receiving end of a complaint honestly want to re-engage with angry customers. Usually they're happy just to get them out of the way. A follow-up call that asks if the problem was addressed satisfactorily will knock most people off their chairs. This tactic is so rarely used that it can quickly turn screaming critics into enthusiastic fans. Unfortunately, few companies expect or reward their people for going the extra mile. Once the transaction is completed or the problem dispatched, it's time to quickly move to the next person in line.

The best way to head off customer dissatisfaction is to empower people on the front lines with the ability to solve problems and to lead by example. Managers who show enthusiasm for customer service and applaud people for going the extra mile inspire others to emulate them.

That may mean a wholesale change in culture defined by a big idea. A few years ago, American Express set an audacious goal to become "the world's most respected business brand." The company sought to recast customer service in a manner that truly put customers at the center. It hired customer service reps from the hospitality, healthcare, retail and airline industries. Then it ditched some of the traditional metrics in favor of customer satisfaction research.

"*Empowering* is a word that is often used but rarely delivered," said Tammy Weinbaum, an Amex senior vice president. "We wanted to give all of our people the power to deliver for their customers. We had to move away from customer service being a cost to being an investment in our business, move away from 'hurry up and get off the phone' to always leaving a favorable lasting impression."

That means breaking the rules, though, and few companies do that willingly. One of our favorite examples of this is Southwest Airlines, which gives its flight attendants the flexibility to have fun while conducting humdrum work like reading the FAA flight safety rules. Paul remembers one petite Southwest attendant who hid in the overhead bin to surprise unsuspecting passengers when they opened it. The stunt got a huge laugh, and travelers talked about it for the entire flight. Can you imagine most airlines tolerating that kind of behavior?

David Holmes, a former personal trainer who joined Southwest in 2005, became an Internet sensation when his hip-hop-inspired rap version of the FAA rules[6] was captured by passengers on their cell phones and spread on YouTube.

Some airlines might have freaked out to hear an employee relate a legal mandate as "If you have a seat on a row with an exit, we're gonna talk to ya so ya might as well expect it," but Southwest did quite the opposite. It invited Holmes to present the Generally Accepted Accounting Principles rules as a "GAAP Rap" at its shareholder meeting, and introduced him as the "rhythmic ambassador of Southwest culture."[7]

The FAA has done nothing to stop Southwest from having fun with the rules. Why should it? Southwest passengers are actually *listening* to something that passengers on most other airlines tune out. Southwest understands that if it can make the flying experience a little less burdensome, then customers will reward it with loyalty. The strategy seems to work, since Southwest is consistently one of the top airlines in both profitability and customer satisfaction.

It's Personal

An analysis of customer attack patterns shows a clear link between poor customer service and online retaliation. Altimeter Group analyzed 50 notable customer attacks and grouped them into 13 categories (some incidents fell into more than one category).[8] Table 1 shows the groupings and reveals some interesting patterns.

In one-third of the cases documented by Altimeter, the attack was initiated by a single customer's poor experience, and nearly 40% of the incidents were rooted in failure to respect the customer. Nearly all of these incidents were preventable if there were more attention paid to processes, training and customer-centric cultural values.

Here are capsule summaries of cases studied by Altimeter. Could any of these happen to your business?[9]

- A restaurant employee scolds a customer for ordering bacon during a religious holiday the restaurant was observing. A recording of the altercation goes viral.

- An airline passenger uploads a video of a flight that held passengers on the tarmac for seven hours. The video goes viral.

- A premium chocolatier heavily marks up secretly repackaged chocolate products. The fraud is exposed on blogs.

- A wife blogs about her husband's excessive work hours, leading to charges of unethical human resources practices against his employer.

- A video of a service technician asleep on a customer's couch goes viral.

- A magazine publishes a recipe from a blog without permission then criticizes the blogger's writing when she complains. Sympathizers attack the magazine's Facebook wall with accusations of copyright violation.

- A company launches a cause marketing campaign but then bombards registrants with product promotions unrelated to the cause.

- A computer maker contracts with six bloggers to review a laptop, promising that the review that generates the most response can keep the product. It then tries to change the rules when the winning review is negative.

If you found yourself shaking your head and mumbling, "What were they *thinking?*" while reading those summaries, we don't blame you. It's amazing how often businesses sacrifice the customer for their own best interests. And that's despite the mountain of statistical evidence that customer service is increasingly the key driver of repeat business, word-of-mouth awareness and customer acquisition.

You have to wonder how any airline could leave passengers sitting on a runway for 30 minutes or more without offering an explanation for the holdup. It's happened to us many times, and we'll bet it's happened to you, too. That's because pilots aren't trained in the importance of customer satisfaction. JetBlue, which experienced a crisis in 2007 in which some of its planes were stalled for hours because of weather problems, now expects pilots to keep passengers personally informed of the cause of a delay. If the holdup is JetBlue's fault, it has gate agents standing by at the destination to distribute discount vouchers to people shuffling off the plane. Imagine how much trouble these modest steps avoid.

Altimeter's research concluded that more than three quarters of the social media-driven crises it studied could have been prevented if the companies had been better prepared. Even among the 18 companies it identified as "advanced" users of social channels, few had a disciplined process to synthesize feedback to improve their products and services. Many of these companies were listening to customers but had internal systems that were incapable of capturing that information in a usable form.

Table 1

Cause of Attack	% of Incidents
A customer has a poor experience not attributable to an individual employee	17%
A customer, who happens to have high influence in a community, is treated badly.	16%
A company broke common ethical practices (for example, trust, transparency, fair competition) in social media	14%
A few employees behaved inappropriately	8%
A company posts inappropriate or controversial content on social media outlets	8%
A company pretends to be something it isn't ("Astroturfing")	7%
Legal guidelines like disclosure or terms and conditions are violated	7%
A company attempts to control a community on social outlets	6%
The attacker is a group promoting a cause (for example, Greenpeace or PETA)	6%
Incorrect information is reported, not necessarily with the company's knowledge	5%
A company fails to respond to a complaint sufficiently and in a timely manner	5%
Other	4%

This lack of continuous improvement is one of the biggest factors that feeds customer dissatisfaction. A customer's complaint may get a receptive ear and a promise to do better, but six months later nothing has changed. That is usually because the company has no process for elevating and aggregating negative feedback. Social media has created a free global focus group, but many companies still don't know what to do with it. Perhaps one of the problems is that the marketing department is still running the show. A March 2012 survey of 329 North American businesses by the Economist Intelligence Unit reported that more than 60% of the companies invest primary social media responsibility in marketing and sales organizations. Less than 6% let customer service lead the charge.[10]

This organizational structure is a holdover from the early days of social media when the new tools were primarily seen as just another marketing channel. Many companies still think that way. Researcher A.T. Kearney, Inc. found that 28 of the world's top 50 brands didn't respond to a single customer comment on their Facebook pages in 2011, the same as in 2010. Far too many companies see social media as just a way to blast a message. They're missing at least half the value.

Satisfaction is Relative

For all the attention we pay to customer satisfaction in this book, we should also point out that absolute satisfaction is neither achievable nor necessarily desirable. The cost may not be worth the benefit. The goal isn't necessarily to make *every* customer happy, but rather to satisfy enough customers to keep your business ahead of the competition.

Barlow and Møller cite research at Case Western Reserve University that revealed an unusually high percentage of active detractors in the automotive repair industry. They theorize that this is because many people are hardwired to expect bad experiences with auto shops either because they've been ripped off in the past or have heard many stories of others who have been cheated. They're trained to expect the worst, so their expectations are lower.

Even the best companies have a minority of dissatisfied customers. Sentiment analysis on public discussions of Apple Computer, for example, consistently shows about 15% to 20% negative comments. That's despite the fact that Apple enjoys an adoring customer base and extraordinarily high overall satisfaction. But even Apple can't please everyone.

Sometimes customer inconvenience can even be a virtue. Consider these unusual scenarios:

- Whenever Apple introduces a new iPhone, TV crews capture video of customers standing in long lines to buy the first units. These images are great PR for Apple because they show people enduring discomfort to be the first on their block with the new phone. However, if those customers were standing outside a bank trying to take their money out, the perception would be quite different.

- There's a restaurant in Boston called Durgin Park that serves some of the best steak and prime rib in New England in a mess-hall atmosphere. While the restaurant has become more customer-friendly in recent years, its long-time reputation was as an uncomfortable place to dine. Patrons sat at long communal tables, ate with institutional silverware and could stand in line for an hour or more waiting for a seat. The waitresses were notoriously nasty. A diner's request was often met with a scowl or an insult. And people traveled from all around New England to eat there.

  Why would a place that seemingly did everything wrong from a customer service perspective attract such rabid fans? Because Durgin Park had hit on a unique formula that worked. The crusty waitresses were part of the floor show. The long lines and institutional setting were the indignities that customers endured to enjoy great prime rib at fast-food prices. Inconvenience was part of the Durgin Park experience, and it gave diners good stories to share.

- Alamo Drafthouse is a chain of boutique theatres for hard-core film lovers. Its strict rules ban customers from talking or texting during movies, and the staff doesn't hesitate to eject patrons for a single offense. This enrages some customers.

In the spring of 2011, one of those displaced patrons left an obscenity-laced diatribe on the theatre's voice mail. Instead of apologizing, Alamo transcribed the message and posted it, uncut, on YouTube. It concluded by thanking the caller for promising never to return to Alamo again.

Alamo Drafthouse knows that the customers it cares about appreciate the attention the theatre pays to making the most of their cinematic experience. Keeping that core group happy is worth pissing off a few people who won't abide by the rules.

- In the early days of Twitter, system outages were so frequent that the cartoon logo on the service's error page came to be affectionately known as the "fail whale." Many online businesses would consider frequent server crashes a nightmare, but Twitter knew the real cause was system overload. So many people wanted to use the service that the technology couldn't handle the demand, and media coverage of the outages actually sparked curiosity about why the service was so desirable. Had the problems continued for too long they could have become a serious problem for Twitter, but in the short term they were a PR bonanza.

You may know a restaurant or ice cream shop that's so popular that people stand in line for hours to eat there. Ordinarily you would say it's terrible to keep customers waiting, but not if demand exceeds supply. As Yogi Berra said about the St. Louis restaurant Ruggeri's, "Nobody goes there anymore. It's too crowded."

Customer satisfaction is contextual to the situation and the industry. Airlines know most passengers are satisfied simply to get to their destination safely and on time for a reasonable fare. Customer service exists to solve problems but isn't expected to delight anyone. People expect to wait in line at Walmart but not at Nordstrom. Diners expect a more pleasant experience at Ruth's

Chris than at Jack in the Box. The value proposition for these businesses is different.

Airlines are interesting examples of customer service extremes. Take Ryanair, the big European carrier based in Dublin. It's famous both for rock-bottom pricing and for a notoriously nasty attitude toward its customers. There are stories of Ryanair refusing to provide wheelchairs for disabled passengers and even floating an idea to charge for use of the lavatory. In August 2011, a Ryanair flight crew reportedly treated a passenger who was having a heart attack by giving him a sandwich and a drink — and then charging him for both (the airline disputes this account).[11]

The U.S. version of Ryanair is Spirit Airlines, a discount carrier whose Google profile reads, "cheap tickets, cheap flights, discount airfare, cheap hotels, cheap car rentals, cheap travel." In 2012, Spirit announced it was raising the fee for carry-on bags to as much as $100 each way. That's right: *carry-on* bags. The company explained it was trying to encourage passengers to check baggage instead of incurring delays by dragging everything onto the plane.[12] However, for a company that charges for everything from sodas to pillows, the fees were widely perceived as simply a way to gouge customers (they were later reduced).

The same week, Spirit also came under fire for refusing to refund the ticket of a veteran who was dying of cancer. Even though the passenger had a doctor's statement saying he was too sick to fly, the airline stuck to its policy for several days until CEO Ben Baldanza eventually relented and paid the refund out of his own pocket. This was in character for Baldanza: Two years earlier he accidentally hit "Reply All" on an e-mail and told two customers who were asking compensation for a delayed flight that the company owed them nothing and they would be back the next time they wanted a low fare.

Few companies can survive with a customer-antagonistic culture, but in rare cases it can be a viable strategy. That doesn't mean, however, that we recommend it.

Chapter 5:
The Attackers

Dave Carroll is one of the nicest guys you'll ever meet. A lanky Canadian with an easy smile and a honey-smooth voice, he seems an unlikely candidate to mount a customer attack. But Carroll's satirical send-up of United Airlines is a classic example of how one person's experience can embarrass a global corporation and trigger policy change across an entire industry.

Dave Carroll

Carroll's story has been widely documented and is described in detail on his website, DaveCarrollMusic.com, so we won't go into detail here. To summarize, he and his country music band, Sons of Maxwell, were beginning a week-long tour of Nebraska in March 2008 when they witnessed United Airlines baggage handlers at Chicago's O'Hare airport tossing their musical instruments around like sacks of potatoes.

Carroll complained to several airline personnel and was told there was nothing they could do. When he arrived in Nebraska he discovered that his $3,500 Taylor guitar had been broken in several places and would require extensive repair, if it could be repaired at all.

Carroll spent the next nine months seeking compensation from United. His quest took him through a gauntlet of procedural absurdity, communication breakdowns and sheer obstinacy that would have frustrated a less-persistent victim, but it was the very runaround that became his sustaining force. He eventually gave up on seeking payment and focused on telling the world his story.

Assault with a Smile

Sons of Maxwell's "United Breaks Guitars" video was created for $150 and debuted on YouTube on July 6, 2009.[1] Carroll's stated goal was to get 1 million views, but that figure was obliterated within a few days. A year and a half later it had been viewed more than 11 million times, and Dave Carroll was a media celebrity with a brisk speaking business and a book about the incident entitled, not surprisingly, *United Breaks Guitars*.

Carroll's campaign was one of the more benign forms of customer attack, but it was effective nonetheless. He made the video only after enduring months of frustration working through official channels, and he went easy on the employees whom he understood were only following orders.

United also responded with restraint. After the video became a viral sensation, the airline offered full restitution, but Carroll declined, saying he was more interested in telling his story than getting a check. Adding insult to injury, when Carroll next flew on United to speak at a RightNow event in Colorado about the video to a room of 1,000 customer service executives, he had to appear in jeans because United had lost his luggage.

United said it has since adopted the video as an internal training tool and has pledged to improve its customer service policies. Other airlines watched the scene from the sidelines and said silent prayers it wasn't them.

Satire is a subtle and pernicious form of customer attack that deserves special attention. While satirical messages may appear harmless, they have tremendous staying power.

One of the earliest and most enduring satirical customer attacks was created by Tom Farmer and Shane Atchison in late 2001 in a PowerPoint presentation called "Yours is a Very Bad Hotel." It described in hilarious detail the experiences of two weary business travelers who arrived at a Doubletree hotel in Houston at 2 a.m. to find that their guaranteed room had been given away. The laconic efforts of desk clerk Mike to secure alternative accommodations provided further hilarity.[2]

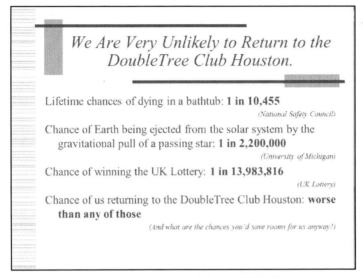

Slide from "Yours is a Very Bad Hotel"

Created before Facebook or YouTube, "Yours is a Very Bad Hotel" spread almost entirely by e-mail. The authors reportedly got more than 5,000 e-mail responses in the week after the slide deck began making the rounds. They also got a $1,000 compensatory donation to charity by the hotel's owner and a promise of "complete retraining of the entire staff," according to *USA Today*.[3] More than a decade later, the presentation still lives on SlideShare, Scribd and numerous other document-sharing sites.

Online attacks take several forms and are driven by different motivations. Compensation is actually rarely the main issue, although for some attackers it is the *only* issue. The vast majority of incidents are driven by the victim's perception that a wrong has been done, the wrongdoer doesn't care about its constituents and the victim speaks for an aggrieved group that can't or won't speak for itself.

Celebrating Your Critics

Many businesses fear online assailants, but we think they should welcome them instead. Vocal complainers are among the tiny percentage of dissatisfied customers who let their opinions be known, and they can be a source of considerable good. After all, they haven't left yet.

That's not true for most people who've had a bad experience. They simply swallow their anger and never return. That's lost business that can never been reclaimed. Only about one in 25 aggrieved customers actually speaks up, estimates Peter Blackshaw, co-founder of Planet Feedback and author of *A Happy Customer Tells Three People, an Unhappy Customer Tells 3,000*. In politics, the ratio is more like one in 100. That's one reason why squeaky wheels get so much attention from politicians: They're assumed to speak for many others. Complainers can be an important source of improvement and even word-of-mouth marketing.

Here's why you should value them:

- **They're trying to help**. While it may not seem that way when the customer across the counter is turning purple, you're getting an offer of support. People who take the time to complain do it because they care. Most just want a receptive ear and a commitment to improve. They complain because they want a conversation.

- **Complainers influence others**. Vocal customers are good at rallying sympathizers. They know how to use the tools of influence, and they're not shy about sharing their opinions. If their attitudes can be turned around — and 90% of the time they can — they are the quickest to tell others about their positive experience. That's why an attacker should never be dismissed.

- **They're early warning signals**. Why would you want to keep a product on the shelf that no one wants or hang on to an employee who's pissing people off? Complainers tell you when you're doing something wrong, which means you can fix the problem faster. Sam Decker, who was founding CMO at social analytics firm Bazaarvoice, notes that some of the greatest value that his company's customers got from online feedback was improved inventory control. They were able to get weak products off the shelves months before the sales reports came in.

Of course, not all angry customers can be satisfied, and some have vendettas or political agendas that can never be resolved. There are also some people who just enjoy stirring up trouble. McDonald's CEO Jim Skinner calls these C.A.V.E. people for "Citizens Against Virtually Everything."[4] You have to know when to cut your losses. But the typical organizational response to attackers, which is either to quiet them or ignore them, fails to take advantage of the true value they offer.

The Four Types of Attacker

Let's look at the four most common profiles of online attackers, which we call Casual Complainers, Extortionists, Committed Crusaders and Indignant Influencers. Each has different motivations and requires different response strategies.

Casual Complainers

Who They Are: They're the background noise of any crowd, the people customer service organizations were created to handle. They've usually had isolated bad experiences that caused irritation but didn't prompt dramatic action. In many cases, they either have little brand loyalty or are captive customers with limited alternatives (think utilities). They grumble but usually don't leave. They deserve to be listened and responded to, but investing significant time and money in satisfying them won't return big rewards.

The airline industry has a lot of Casual Complainers. Nobody likes to fly, and most frequent travelers have had so many bad experiences that they no longer have much affinity to any brand. The flying public's overall expectations are so low that complaints are part of everyday conversation.

Banks, utilities and government agencies also have a lot of Casual Complainers. Their customers either can't or won't take the trouble to switch. Dissatisfaction levels are high, but dealing with each and every complaint of this type usually isn't worth the trouble.

Response Strategy: The best way to deal with Casual Complainers is through policies. Empower people who deal directly with customers to handle common problems with consistent and fair responses that are crafted with customer satisfaction in mind.

Unfortunately, many of the organizations that have a lot of Casual Complainers use policies that protect the organization rather than please the customer. Policies like these can actually make the problem worse. Dave Carroll never denied that United representatives followed policy in dealing with his problem. His complaint was that the policies themselves were ridiculous. Procedures that palm off disaffected customers on other departments, introduce delay or contribute to frustration can turn a dispute into a shouting match.

Some companies have strategies that blunt attacks by giving the customer ultimate control. L.L. Bean, Land's End and Coach are examples of firms that promise no-questions-asked refunds, repairs or replacements if the customer is dissatisfied with any product. The secret of this policy is that few customers ever take advantage of the guarantees unless they really need to. In fact, the guarantees actually reduce costs because customer service reps don't have to deal with every complaint.

JetBlue has a core set of principles that gives employees considerable latitude to satisfy complaints on the spot without running through a gauntlet of approvals. The airline understands that it's cheaper to over-compensate the exception than to micromanage the rule.

The airline also encourages everyone to interact with customers when possible. "It's not unheard of to see the pilot in the gate area with a laptop, showing customers the weather map and explaining why there is a delay, even though the sun is shining where they are," said Jenny Dervin, vice president of corporate communications at JetBlue. That transparency cuts off complaints before they start.

Extortionists

Who They Are: Extortionists are motivated by personal gain, which makes them the most irritating breed of attacker. They also present some unique management challenges. We don't categorize your run-of-the-mill refund-seekers as Extortionists. These people are after bigger rewards, whether it be free stuff, damages or excessive compensation.

Extortionists need to be evaluated individually because their campaigns are often rooted in reasonable complaints, but greed has escalated their demands to unreasonable levels. Paul worked with one durable-goods client that was struggling with a customer who complained that defects in the company's products had sabotaged an entire home improvement project. The client had already replaced the products the customer had bought with a higher-grade stock, but the man was demanding more than $12,000 in additional compensation for his trouble. He was airing his complaints in every online forum he could find and increasing his demands as time went on. Paul's advice: Let the man rant. As long as the supplier had made reasonable efforts to compensate him — and was willing to outline those efforts if pressed — it had sufficient deniability.

Other Extortionists are more opportunistic. They may use the promise of negative reviews on online ratings sites or the threat of a hate blog to try to extract rewards. In 2011, *The Week* reported on the growing concerns of hotel and restaurant owners in the U.K. over customers who threatened to attack their businesses on the influential TripAdvisor travel reviews site if they didn't get room upgrades and free meals.[5] "One B&B owner who felt 'coerced' into giving two customers their money back says the travel website has become a 'monster,'" the newspaper reported. Many business owners in other industries have told us the same thing anecdotally.

Response Strategy: Think precedent. Evaluate the Extortionist's case, and decide if compensation is warranted in line with your standard practices. Remember that you are setting a precedent.

Don't fall into the trap of giving away the farm just to get rid of them. Extortionists like to complain publicly, and they're only too happy to tell others about the generous reward they got. The next time an Extortionist attacks you'll be expected to do the same thing. And the next time and the next.

Over-compensating an Extortionist can also make the problem worse. If the attacker is convinced that your company is evil, then a large payout will simply reinforce the suspicion that you have something to hide. You'll have an even bigger problem on your hands.

When confronted with an Extortionist online, immediately move the conversation offline. Never negotiate in public. The reality is that even your offline discussions are likely to be disclosed by your attacker, but at least don't make that your decision.

Don't increase your offer beyond that which you believe is fair. If the attacks continue and are drawing attention, be ready to respond in a blog, press release or prepared statement that you made a good faith effort to negotiate and that going any further would be unfair to the many customers with whom you enjoy an excellent relationship. When it becomes clear that nothing is going to defuse the situation, be prepared to walk away. Most Extortionists know when they've reached the point of diminishing returns and it's time to move on to another victim.

If a customer threatens you with a negative review, state the consequences. Tell him that credible review sites do not tolerate blackmail and that you're obligated to report his threats to the website operator if he carries through on them. Be ready to do exactly that. Operators of review sites are just as interested as you are in preventing abuse.

If a punitive review appears, respond only to the facts. Avoid accusations and character assassination. Don't reveal that you were threatened unless you have supporting documentation like e-mails. Remember that the sympathy vote automatically goes to the customer, so people will tend to regard your protests as self-serving or worse. Take the high road, even when your instincts tell you otherwise. Confront your accuser only when you're out of choices (see sidebar, "Should You Ever Go Negative?").

Committed Crusaders

Who they are: These are the most persistent breed of attacker and often the most successful. They're motivated by a higher callings, such as the environment, human or animal rights, public health and consumer rights, and their causes are frequently noble, if not always realistic. Committed Crusaders can be tireless in their pursuit of what they believe, and they're good at building armies of followers. They run the gamut from individuals to global organizations. Pampers nemesis Rosana Shah is a Committed Crusader. So is Greenpeace. Change.org is full of their petitions.

Committed Crusaders are usually smart, cool and savvy about how to apply the many tools available to them. They know their cause and their enemies. They look for every opportunity to press their case or to catch their foe in a lie or inconsistency. When momentum is on their side, they can be very effective. Committed Cusaders successfully reversed public attitudes toward smoking, refocused the auto industry on energy-efficient vehicles and forced fast-food chains to embrace healthier menus.

Kristen Christian is a Committed Crusader. In October 2011, she became incensed by a $5 surcharge that appeared on her Bank of America statement for use of the bank's automated teller machines. The Los Angeles-based art gallery owner reasoned that ATMs saved banks money and that charging customers to use them was both unfair and greedy.

Christian took her cause to Facebook, asking her 500 friends to move their money from big banks to credit unions. Friends shared her message with others, and one woman's cause quickly became a movement called Bank Transfer Day, sparking rallies and even marches.

On the other side of the country, 22-year-old recent college graduate Molly Katchpole was also taking up the cause. She went to Change.org and asked people to support her petition calling on

Bank of America to reverse the fee. The media showed interest, so Katchpole staged a protest by cutting up her debit card in front of the television cameras. She also moved her $2,200 in savings to a community bank.

The co-incident campaigns launched by two women who had never met became a nightmare for the country's second-largest bank and a windfall for small credit unions. The media ate up the classic David vs. Goliath story. Christian was interviewed by CNN, Dan Rather Reports, Fox Business, ABC World News, National Public Radio, *The Los Angeles Times* and dozens of other outlets.

Katchpole's Change.org petition attracted more than 300,000 signatures. Bank of America quickly caved in. It had no choice. The Credit Union National Association, a trade organization, estimated that 650,000 Americans opened credit union accounts in the month following the announcement of the debit card fee, about eight times the average rate. Its chief executive told the *Los Angeles Times*: "I think we may look back in a few years and say that this was the spark that caused a lot of people to say, 'Yes, credit unions are a better deal.'"[6]

Katchpole wasn't finished. Two months later, Verizon Corp. quietly began charging a $2 fee to customers who paid their bills online. The Twittersphere grumbled, but Katchpole took action. She returned to Change.org, where her petition gathered 166,000 signatures and a quick reversal by the carrier. Three months later, *Time* magazine included her in its list of the 100 most influential people in America.[7] At 22 years old.

Committed Crusaders are tenacious, and you should never underestimate their will. Giving such a critic a coupon or a free checking account is an insult. Bank of America and Verizon ultimately realized that resisting Committed Crusaders would be more damaging to their image in the long run than giving in.

Not so with Nestlé. In early 2010, Greenpeace launched a Facebook campaign against the Swiss chocolatier's use of palm oil, which it charged was contributing to the devastation of rain forests.

Supporters took their cause to the Nestlé Facebook page, posting hundreds of derogatory messages.

Nestlé panicked and responded by deleting some of the most critical posts, citing misuse of the company's trademarks in altered logos some of the attackers had created. This only made matters worse. Protesters charged that Nestlé was using the intellectual property argument to censor critics. A Nestlé administrator didn't make the situation any better by posting arrogant comments such as "Thanks for the lesson in manners. Consider yourself embraced. But it's our page, we set the rules, it was ever thus."[8]

The confrontation boiled over into mainstream media, where media critics and First Amendment activists joined environmentalists in piling on until the company sheepishly admitted its mistake and allowed the negative comments to stand. Two years later the Nestlé dispute was still being held up as an example of what *not* to do when customers attack.

Response Strategy: Always treat Committed Crusaders with respect. Their causes may be driven by ideology, but they often have good reason for their opinions. You're not going to persuade them to change their views, so focus on the facts, fight on your own turf and rally sympathizers to your side. Committed Crusaders often align themselves with controversial issues, so consider whether it's even worth negotiating with them. If they aren't the type of people who would ever buy your product in the first place, then agreeing to disagree may be the best strategy.

Censoring them won't work. If you bar the gate, they'll get angrier and go somewhere else. The Internet has become a giant whack-a-mole game, and it's pointless to try to bury your foes.

Committed Crusaders won't hesitate to use every tool at their disposal, from hate sites to video to public demonstrations. It's important to know three things:

A Committed Crusader Speaks

Kristen Christian's Bank Transfer Day campaign started with 500 Facebook friends and became a national movement. In an e-mail interview, she spoke of her motivations.

Why did you decide to take your cause online?

I learned from a Wikipedia article that not-for-profit credit unions use profits from my banking business to support local charities and offer low-interest loans to individuals and small businesses. Realizing that financial cooperatives offer an opportunity to turn our nation's economy around, I reached out to my social circle in the second language of Millennials: Facebook.

When did you realize that the movement had a life of its own?

Within three days, the original Facebook event had 10,000 RSVPs from people planning to attend. I got a call from a reporter for the *Village Voice*. I thought, "Why would the *Village Voice* want to talk to me?" But that was just the beginning. My life was turned upside down during the next month. I spent my days responding to hundreds of contacts from supporters each day and conducting interviews with nearly every major media network. Despite the small sacrifice of comfort and privacy, I felt fortunate to have an opportunity to share this powerful message.

How did Bank of America respond?

Bank of America has not responded to me regarding the end of our 15-year banking relationship or the Bank Transfer Day initiative.

What did you learn from this experience?

I've always believed in our moral obligation to stand up for what we believe in. While I'm humbled at how many Americans chose to follow my initiative, I can't take credit for Bank Transfer Day. Without the support of everyone, it wouldn't have been possible.

- What do they want?

- What will they accept?

- What is the opportunity cost of making them go away?

If a Committed Crusader's cause has merit and is generating a lot of public sympathy, then consider meeting some demands. It would have been foolish, for example, for McDonald's to continue to push a fat-laden menu in the face of a documented national obesity epidemic and demands for healthier alternatives. It also would have been bad for business. Giving in to critics isn't a bad thing if it's the right thing to do. In fact, you usually get brownie points for being willing to change.

Some situations are best handled with grudging coexistence. Walmart has been the target of adversarial groups for more than a decade. The Making Change At Walmart campaign organized by the United Food and Commercial Workers has been a constant critic of the retailer's employment practices. Its website meticulously documents news, legal actions and media commentary that reflect badly on the company. This group must irritate Walmart, but the retailer has chosen to live with the pain rather than make the expensive reforms the group demands. That's a business decision.

In some cases, negotiation may not even be in your best interest, particularly when the attackers are never going to be customers. In an example from a few years ago, General Motors ran a consumer-generated video campaign for its Chevy Tahoe SUV in 2006 that was hijacked by environmentalists who used the tools GM provided to blast the company's environmental record. The campaign was widely perceived to be a PR disaster, but from a brand awareness and sales perspective it was a home run.

Wired reported that the Tahoe hit a record 30% market share the month after the ad ran and that average sales cycles dropped to 46 days from nearly four months a year earlier.[9] It turns out criticism from a group that would never consider buying the SUV in the first place wasn't a problem for GM, and it even may have motivated some SUV enthusiasts to show support with a purchase.

Committed Crusaders are worthy adversaries who should never be underestimated. Pay them respect because they just might be right.

Indignant Influencers

Who They Are: When an attack explodes out of nowhere, there's usually an Indignant Influencer at the center. This group includes actors, athletes, politicians, columnists and even notable bloggers. They're basically people who have a built-in following, which means their run-in with your customer service rep or frustration with a defective product can generate a conversation among millions of people regardless of whether there's a bigger problem there. On the other hand, they can also be devastatingly effective if their cause has merit.

Some of the most famous customer attacks have been at the hands of Indignant Influencers. In 2006, media critic and prominent blogger Jeff Jarvis told of his frustrations with his Dell computer in a blog post titled "Dell Hell" that sparked a torrent of me-too comments from other Dell customers and ultimately contributed to an overhaul of Dell's customer support operations.

In February 2011, prominent director Kevin Smith was denied seating on a Southwest Airlines flight because the plane lacked two adjacent seats to accommodate his 300-pound frame. Smith took his cause to Twitter and harangued the airline for days. The story provoked a national discussion about the obligation of institutions to accommodate obese customers and whether Smith's complaint was justified. Southwest, which was simply following a policy practiced by most airlines, responded with a tight-lipped smile but refused to change its rules.

In December of that year, actor Alec Baldwin was tossed off an American Airlines flight for refusing to turn off his smart phone and locking himself in the lavatory while passengers waited to take off. There was no question that Baldwin's antics were inappropriate, but the situation was a PR distraction for the airline and it inflamed a public debate about the FAA's electronic device rule that airlines would just as soon avoid discussing.

In most cases, Indignant Influencers abandon their campaigns pretty quickly if offered an explanation, apology or a reasonable makegood. They're usually busy people who have more pressing demands on their time than pillorying a business.

Responding with self-deprecating humor can be an effective tactic if the slight isn't too extreme, like United Airlines adopting "United Breaks Guitars" for customer service training. If self-effacing humor isn't an option, get the dispute out of the public eye as quickly as possible. Be careful of overreaction, however. You should never change a policy because of one complaint, even if that person has an Academy Award.

There may be more to an Indignant Influencer's campaign than meets the eye. An influencer who cultivates an image as a rogue may see a run-in with a respected brand as an irresistible promotional opportunity. Baldwin made his ejection from an American Airlines flight a running gag in TV ads and appearances for months after the incident.

Even an influencer with a legitimate ax to grind may get collateral value from pressing a campaign. In 2007, Bob Garfield put up a website called "Comcast Must Die" to protest what he maintained was lousy customer service from the cable provider. Garfield is no ordinary pissed-off consumer. He's a columnist for *Advertising Age*, an author and co-host of National Public Radio's "On the Media" program.

ComcastMustDie.com was both an expression of Garfield's frustration and an invitation for others to vent. He stoked the fires online and through his media channels, including *Ad Age*. Comcast desperately tried to satisfy him – at one point sending five trucks to his neighborhood to troubleshoot the problem – but Garfield said his agenda was much bigger.

"Their sudden attentiveness implied that my jihad was just 'blog-mail,' an extortion attempt to get my phones attended to," he wrote in *The Chaos Scenario*. "But it was no such thing. Comcast Must Die was an extortion attempt to get *everybody's* phones attended to."

There's no question Garfield's anger was real, but there were side benefits to him as well. The experience provided fodder for his media programs. It was a proof-of-concept for a central point of his book, which is that the Internet changes the balance of power. It even helped burnish his image as a lovable rogue.

In the end, Comcast announced significant revisions to its customer service policies, including a procedure for monitoring Internet traffic for complaints. Paraphrasing a famous quote, Garfield wrote, "Never pick a fight with someone who buys zeros and ones by the barrel. Which, nowadays, is everyone." Bad behavior can have its rewards.

What can we learn from these run-ins with Indignant Influencers? One lesson is that they have the capacity to incite large numbers of people to voice their complaints that might otherwise be locked up. They're classic fire-starters. Another is that their actions may have as much to do with advancing a personal agenda as with righting a wrong.

The challenge for communicators is to keep calm when the situation seems to be spiraling out of control. Unless there's evidence that the Indignant Influencer has unlocked a wellspring of ill will, it's likely that the situation will blow over pretty quickly. Taking your lumps with a grin is often the best course.

But don't let the Indignant Influencer light a match. Comcast made a mistake in believing it had a problem with Garfield. In fact, it had a problem with thousands of customers who were moved by a prominent influencer to make their opinions known. Comcast's efforts to overcompensate in fixing Garfield's problem looked desperate. It actually made the situation worse.

American Airlines handled the Baldwin case more adroitly. It realized that customers were more likely to sympathize with the flyers who had been inconvenienced by the actor's antics and that its adherence to a government policy was entirely appropriate. Baldwin may have been able to make light of the incident but not at American's expense. It was one of those rare attacks in which both sides came out looking pretty good.

Styles of Attack

Barlow and Møller also group disgruntled customers into four categories, but they organize them by the way they express displeasure.[10] It's another useful way to look at the problem. Percentages refer to their estimate of the percent of customers in each category.

- **Voicers** (37%) are eager to help a company improve its products and services. They generally complain directly to the company. They are the best critics you can ask for.

- **Passives** (14%) continue doing business with the company but with no enthusiasm. They don't tell many people about their experiences, and when they do, their opinions are neutral. Passives can sometimes do substantial damage when they reach the boiling point, but most simply suffer in silence. Utilities have lots of passive customers.

- **Irates** (21%) don't complain to the company, but they do complain to other people. While they lack the determination to become activists, they can be dangerous in groups. Listen in on a group of seasoned travelers, and you'll hear Irates in action. Given a sympathetic audience, they let loose.

- **Activists** (28%) "are potentially the most lethal of the four groups," Barlow and Møller write. "They may be seeking revenge while spreading the word of the company's bad service to everyone and never again patronizing the company. Activists can even damage a company's stock price." Most Committed Crusaders are Activists and are responsible for some of the most damaging attacks.

Activists typically comprise only about 4% of all complainers, but the energy they bring to their crusade more than makes up for their numbers. They've already decided never to do business with the company again, but their goals are more ambitious. They may seek humiliation, financial damage or prosecution.

People don't become Activists overnight, Barlow and Møller explain. Their dissatisfaction is fueled by frustration with normal channels of complaint and the perception that the company doesn't care. Some organizations dedicated to causes, such as People for the Ethical Treatment of Animals (PETA) and Greenpeace, are essentially professional Activists. They don't do business with the companies they attack and never will. They aren't satisfied with anything less than an abandonment of current practices or significant damage to the company.

It's almost impossible to mollify people once they've crossed over the Activist threshold. Use our advice for handling Committed Crusaders as the foundation of your strategy.

Should You Ever Go Negative?

In October 2009, the U.S. Transportation Security Administration was the victim of a blogger attack. A young mother named Nicole White posted an entry on her blog accusing TSA personnel of detaining her for more than 45 minutes at Atlanta's Hartsfield Airport, separating her from her infant son and conducting an unreasonable and invasive body search.[11]

The accusations were a potential bombshell for the TSA, whose unpleasant but necessary task makes it one of the least-popular government agencies. But the agency had a course of response. Officials immediately retrieved the security tapes of the incident and examined them. The tapes showed that none of the blogger's allegations was true. Her detention had lasted nine minutes, she had never been separated from her child and the search was done by the book.

TSA took a gamble. The same evening the accusations appeared on White's blog, the agency posted the videos on The TSA Blog.[12] The comeback post, written by "Blogger Bob," was tasteful and respectful. Bob noted that as a parent of two small children, he sympathized with the anxiety of the mother, but the evidence showed that White's accusations were wildly exaggerated.

The agency assembled a nine-minute video compilation of clips taken from different security cameras. It also posted the full video from each camera. "You'll see the video clearly shows that this individual was never separated from her baby by TSA," Blogger Bob wrote. "You'll also see that a lot of the other claims are also unfounded."

The bet paid off. White's accusations had already generated considerable buzz online. Reporters were calling, and MSNBC was reportedly preparing to feature the story the next day. Given the level of public hostility that already existed toward the agency, there was a risk that the story could spin out of control into a series of "he said/she said" accusations.

By posting the videos, the TSA successfully turned the tide away from the blogger's charges and toward its own innocence. Its counterattack became the bigger story, and most of the media coverage was sympathetic to the agency. White, whose blog acknowledges a "lifelong history of severe anxiety," admitted in a follow-up post that the video contradicted much of her story.

Despite the fact that the video evidence was incontrovertible, the TSA still came in for criticism. More than 450 comments were submitted to its blog. While most supported the agency, a substantial minority found fault either with the videos or the procedures they depicted. Some even accused the agency of falsifying evidence.

The TSA's counterattack was the riskiest form of response. Counterattacks work only if there is incontrovertible evidence that the attacker is either lying or flagrantly disregarding the facts. Even then, a skeptical public may still look for ways to side with the aggrieved individual. The larger the counterattacking entity is, the less sympathy it gets.

Experienced crisis communicators always recommend taking the high road, sticking to the facts and resisting the urge to counterattack. But sometimes there's no choice. If you have to take on an aggressor, keep these guidelines in mind:

- **Play defense.** Your goal is to generate sympathy and protect your reputation, not to harm anyone.

- **Don't make it personal**. Address facts, not individuals. Avoid making subjective judgments.

- **Be respectful.** Never insult an attacker, no matter how outrageous his claims may be. The TSA's Blogger Bob was careful to show sympathy for the mother's anxiety before refuting her claims.

- **Don't speculate**. It has no place in crisis communications. Statements like, "It could never happen here," will backfire on you if it turns out that it did.

- **Be sure your evidence is unassailable**. In the age of Photoshop, we can't even believe our eyes anymore. Airtight evidence must come from credible sources and stand up to charges of manipulation. If it's your word against an assailant's, you'll lose.

- **Test your strategy**. Enlist a friendly but dispassionate third party, such as your PR counsel or a business partner, to shoot holes in your counterattack. Test for every possible weakness because you can be sure your opponents will.

Remember that counterattacks usually make the problem worse. If you choose this course, get commitment from the highest levels of the organization because your reputation really will be on the line.

Chapter 6: Ordnance

ord•nance (noun) \ ˈȯrd-nən(t)s\ Military supplies including weapons, ammunition, combat vehicles, and maintenance tools and equipment.

— Merriam-Webster dictionary

Social media has unquestionably been the most potent driving force behind the growing incidence of customer attacks in recent years. Campaigns that once used to require armies of volunteers writing letters, lobbying media and organizing protests are now conducted with hash tags and Facebook pages. Petitions no longer have to be fielded in shopping malls; collecting signatures is as simple as convincing people to click a button. Critics can organize global campaigns without changing out of their pajamas.

We're still in the very early stages of understanding how this all changes relationships between organizations and their constituents. The new economies of scale and velocity require us to discard some old assumptions.

For one thing, the ease with which campaigns are organized today can make them look bigger than they really are. A decade ago, a petition with 50,000 signatures demanded attention. Today, the Change.org petition site hosts scores of active petitions that have many more signatures than that. Does today's online petition merit as much attention as one that was fielded with shoe leather and pencils just a few years ago?

Then there's the time factor. Because attacks can form so quickly, organizations under attack feel pressured to respond in kind, but decisions made in haste are rarely the best ones. Our expectations are rooted in a time when things unfolded much more slowly and raising one's voice required time and commitment. We assumed that a few vocal critics represented many more silent ones. Today, that may not be the case, but our response reflex hasn't yet adapted.

Finally, the rules of interaction have changed. Just five years ago it was almost unheard of for a company to invite its critics to vent their anger in an open forum bearing its brand. Today, that's the cost of being on Facebook. Few organizations are culturally prepared for this kind of transparency, but it's clear we're not going back to the old days. Complete openness demands that we change our assumptions about how we deal with our constituents.

Start by understanding the tools that critics use. An angry customer has an unprecedented arsenal of communications weaponry available, most of it at little or no cost. Each has its own strengths and weaknesses. In this chapter, we examine the tools that attackers use, running down the list in alphabetical order.

Blogs — They Still Matter

The most mature form of social media, blogs have found their niche as a long-form communications tool that's well suited to analysis and exposition. Some of the most famous customer attacks, including Jeff Jarvis' "Dell Hell,"[1] Vincent Ferrari's AOL cancellation[2] and Bob Garfield's "Comcast Must Die" started on blogs. However, recently the popularity of blogging has been eclipsed by social networks, which are simpler to use and come with a built-in audience.

Corporate blogging is in decline. The Center for Marketing Research at the University of Massachusetts at Dartmouth documented a decrease in blogs maintained by both the Inc. 500 and Fortune 500 companies in 2011,[3] the first downturn in the study's five-year history. However, declining corporate interest in blogs is probably due to the fact that it's simply easier to use Twitter or Facebook.

Among enthusiasts and professionals, blogs continue to serve a vital function. Technorati's 2011 State of the Blogosphere survey of more than 4,000 bloggers found that 45% of them have been blogging for more than four years and that the average blogger maintains three blogs.[4] Forty percent of respondents said they blog more than three hours per week. Nearly 80% have a college degree.

In contrast to the idle chatter you find on Facebook or Twitter, blogs are usually serious discussion.

Seven in 10 survey respondents said they blog to gain professional recognition, and 68% said they do it to attract new business. More than two-thirds said they believe blogs are being taken more seriously as sources of information.

Blogs permit more creative latitude than any other medium, and they can be a pretty powerful tool in the hands of a good writer. For a lot of big brands, bloggers are now respected channels to their customers and are important sources of information. Among the brands that regularly host blogger events or have formal influencer relations programs are Procter & Gamble, General Mills, Molson, PepsiCo and Ford Motor Co. General Mills has a members-only club called MyBlogSpark.com, where invited bloggers can get inside information and early access to new products. Software giant SAP has hosted an international conference called the Influencer Summit for several years to cultivate technology bloggers.

Bottom line: Blogging has matured and so have bloggers. Today's bloggers are more committed, more serious and more knowledgeable than the dabblers of a few years ago. Blogs don't amplify an attack as much as social networks do, but they aggregate and analyze better than any other form of social media.

Blogs are also notable for their influence on mainstream media. Every major newspaper hosts contract bloggers, and major news sources such as The Huffington Post, TechCrunch, Daily Beast, Engadget, The Consumerist and The Politico are, in effect, built on blogging platforms or feature the work of prominent bloggers. Journalists looking for experts go first to Google, which favors bloggers for their focus and distinctive voice.

One individual with a blog can gain considerable prominence in a specific topic. For example, Paul has written a blog called Newspaper Death Watch, which chronicles the changes in the newspaper industry, since 2007. The site is a top Google result for many search terms related to the state of newspapers, and Paul has been interviewed or cited by *The New York Times, The Economist, The New*

Yorker, NPR, the Al Jazeera television network and many other outlets as a result. He gets a couple of inquiries a week from reporters or professional journalists seeking his opinion, and the site draws about 500 visitors a day, all because Google deems his content to be useful to his narrow readership. There are thousands of other examples just like this.

In certain industries, blogs are now seen as equivalent in influence to mainstream media. The annual BlogHer conference is a major venue for consumer packaged goods companies to announce new products and curry the favor of influential mom bloggers. General Mills has chosen diet blogger Lisa Lillien of Hungry-Girl.com to announce several of its new products. "She's one of the most cogent voices in the weight management field," said public relations manager David Witt.[5]

We hope we've made our point by now: Bloggers are a major factor to contend with, and in many industries we believe they deserve as much attention as mainstream news outlets. When they mass for an attack — as they did in the Motrin Moms or Komen for the Cure cases — they can catalyze other social media channels and legitimize an issue for mainstream media. Serious bloggers should be treated with respect and given access to your most knowledgeable people.

Change.org — Frictionless Protest

This online petition site has quietly become one of the Internet's most influential voices for change, with membership expected to exceed 25 million by the end of 2012. Described as "one of the most influential channels for activism in the country" by *The Washington Post*, it is capturing the attention of everyone from presidents to PR people.

"[A]nyone, anywhere — from Chicago to Cape Town — can start their own grassroots campaign for change using our organizing platform," Change.org says on its description page. "Your campaign can be about anything from supporting curbside recycling programs to fighting wrongful deportation to protecting against anti-gay bullying." The service is particularly popular in campaigns that involve the environment, human or animal rights, health and consumer advocacy. But some of its biggest successes have related to more prosaic causes, such as hidden fees or product ingredients. Change.org has been criticized for its business model, which sells petition signers' e-mail addresses, but that doesn't seem to be slowing its momentum.

There are several other online petition sites, including PetitionBuzz.com, Care2.com, iPetition.com and SignOn.org. However, Change.org has the most momentum. Starting a petition is as simple as filling out a short Web form, and about 10,000 new petitions are started each month. They range from popular political causes, such as ending human rights abuses in Myanmar, to highly localized and specific issues, such as a plea for the St. Michael Catholic Academy of Austin, Texas, to allow more students to use a shaded grassy area on hot days. Most petitions go nowhere, but a few attract significant attention.

The largest petition ever started on Change.org was filed by the parents of Trayvon Martin, the 17-year-old Florida youth who was shot and killed by a self-appointed neighborhood watch leader in February 2012. It amassed more than 2.3 million signatures in less than three months.[6] Whether the petition played any role in the ultimate arrest of the shooter and resignation of the police chief in the case is hard to tell, but there's no question that it was a catalyst for awareness.

Petition signers can easily notify their social networks of causes they support through automatic links to Facebook, Twitter and e-mail address books, and the site makes it easy to embed an advocacy badge on a website or blog. Change.org also has a detailed guide on how to promote petitions, including tips on the finer points of posting to Twitter and the basics of influencer relations.

Change.org maintains a running list of news stories related to its petitions, and the site stamps a "Victory" ribbon on those that succeed. Two of its most notable successes are Molly Katchpole's protests against Bank of America and Verizon that we described in Chapter 5.

"The way forward is through better storytelling," wrote Jonathan Alter in an essay about Change.org. "Online campaigns work best when they have narratives behind them — plucky stories of average people crowd-sourcing their way to power, as Katchpole did against Bank of America."[7] It so happens that mainstream media outlets look for some of the same features, which is why Change.org is a popular hangout for journalists.

There are no hard and fast rules for how to respond to a Change.org petition. Some drives have gathered more than 180,000 signatures and gone nowhere, while others have forced change with just a few thousand names. However, business leaders should be aware of the growing influence of the site and should keep a watchful eye on their Google Alerts for mention of their name or names of competitors with the Change.org domain. With plans to expand to more than 20 countries by the end of 2012, the site appears to be a force to be reckoned with for the long term.

Consumer Advocacy Sites

"Million-Miler Sues United For Being Downgraded To Second-Tier Status"

"Shuttered Best Buy Puts Illinois Town $200K Deeper Into Debt"

"Walmart Store Has No Room for Veterans On Memorial Day Weekend"

"Many Insurers Changing Prescription Categories So Customers Pay More for Already Expensive Meds"

Readers of The Consumerist (Consumerist.com) may recognize those headlines as typical of the advocacy site, which has posted thousands of experiences submitted by its readers since late 2005. The four above all appeared on a single day: May 29, 2012.

The Consumerist is the best-known example of a genre of pro-consumer websites that includes titles like My3Cents.com, RipoffReport.com, FightBack.com and TheSqueakyWheel.com. In its own way, each fights for the little guy in the ongoing battle against big-box retailers, airlines, fast food restaurants and other businesses people love to hate.

Most use the same formula: Consumers can submit stories about experiences they've had (usually negative), which are then categorized by industry or company. In some cases, facts are checked, but usually the site operators lack the resources to verify much. Liability is managed through disclaimers that put the onus of truth on the contributor.

One of the largest such sites — Ripoff Report — has actually turned disputes between consumers and companies into a revenue stream. The site has more than 675,000 consumer complaints in its database, and its policy is never to remove any of them. Companies that believe their reputations have been sullied can submit a rebuttal, but they also have the option to pay Ripoff Report to act as a mediator between complainant and accused. This policy is controversial, to say the least, but Ripoff Report has never shied from controversy. It's been sued dozens of times.[8]

Consumer advocacy sites have been around for more than a decade, but they were mostly ignored by businesses in their early years. All that has changed, though, as new word-of-mouth channels have emerged to amplify messages.

Ben Popken had a lot to do with that. The editor of The Consumerist from its early days until late 2011, he oversaw an evolution both in the site's advocacy role and in its responsibility to the brands it took on.

Now a Brooklyn, N.Y.-based freelance writer, he speaks of what he learned from his years as a consumer advocate. "People wanted to vent. They wanted to know there was somebody out there who wasn't a robot or a hold signal," he said. "We built an incredible community where a story might immediately draw dozens or hundreds of comments from others with advice."

At first, most brands reacted to The Consumerist with indifference, but that changed "because we were giving companies such a spanking that they had to notice us," Popken said. "Companies learned they couldn't just sit around; they had to act quickly. Every company now seems to have someone who monitors Twitter or the Internet to put out fires before they become the next big story on Consumerist or NBC News."

The Consumerist's approach to its mission has evolved from the early days, when most reports were published with little verification. "As our reputation grew, we realized that if we were going to be taken seriously, we had to give [the companies people complained about] a sporting chance," Popken said. Since its acquisition by Consumer Reports in 2008, The Consumerist has become more vigilant about verifying complaints and seeking response.

Popken is proud of The Consumerist's role in breaking some major stories. It was the first site to draw attention to America Online's famously high-pressure customer retention policies, and it published a well-regarded series of investigations into "cash for gold" operations that buy jewelry from desperate sellers at far less than market value.

The Consumerist coined the term "grocery shrink ray" to describe the practice by which some packaged food makers quietly reduce package size without changing price. It also invented the "executive e-mail carpet bomb," in which consumers derive e-mail addresses of top executives from public sources and deliver large numbers of complaint letters directly to senior management. "It's incredibly effective because the people at the top are often so disconnected from their customers," Popken explained.

Perhaps the greatest endorsement for the value of unfiltered customer feedback as practiced by consumer advocacy sites is the Consumer Products Safety Commission (CPSC), which in early 2011 introduced SaferProducts.gov, a public database that publicizes complaints about safety problems involving any of the 15,000 kinds of consumer goods it regulates.

The respected government agency's approach to quality control is strikingly similar to Ripoff Report's. The CPSC doesn't apply any formal review process to the reports consumers post. Companies that disagree with reviews can post responses but not take down the original complaints. A spokesman said the service has been a valuable source of guidance to the agency in deciding which safety issues to pursue. "Consumers are helping us focus on those things that really matter to them," said Alex Filip, deputy director of the Office of Communications.

Facebook — Prepare to Engage

Facebook is the place to be for most brands these days, but it's also the place to be attacked. Many of the biggest social media-driven crises of the last few years have been driven, or substantially influenced, by Facebook.

As we noted in the introduction, Facebook can be a risky proposition. If you set up a page and permit visitors to post to it, be prepared for complaints. You're a facilitator, not an editor, so don't try to control what people say beyond the basic standards of decency.

A well-crafted Facebook policy is important to avoid the kind of no-win situation in which Nestlé found itself in the palm oil debacle detailed in Chapter 5. If your policy is to permit negative comments to stand, then be ready to accept the consequences. If you explicitly bar negativity, then you'll have fewer fans and productive conversations with your customers. Censorship is an invitation to disaster. Successful brands have learned to not only live with complaints but embrace them in the spirit of improvement. They know that receptivity is good for their image.

Even if you don't have a Facebook page, your brand may still be represented there. Critics can set up pages, too. While that isn't necessarily a problem for you (there are hundreds of "Walmart sucks" pages, for example, but nearly all are empty), a lightly trafficked hate page can become a lightning rod when triggered by an event or negative news report. Facebook comments are a bounty for journalists who use them to seek quotable critics.

Each Facebook page has one or more administrators, some of them identified and some not. If a hate page pops up targeting your brand, don't panic. It probably won't go very far. If you do notice regular activity, it's a good idea to attempt to contact the administrators. Let them know you're watching, and you might even befriend them.

Never threaten or lecture these people. You have no leverage over them, and anything you say is likely to be republished if it can embarrass you. Make an earnest attempt to establish a dialogue out of public view. If they decline to engage, find out everything you can about them in case you're ever forced into a confrontation.

The marketers at ChapStick evidently didn't learn from Nestlé's experience. In 2011, the lip balm maker launched an edgy ad campaign that included a photo of a woman searching behind her sofa, apparently for her ChapStick. The photo was taken from the rear, and some people considered the image to be sexist and demeaning. They took their protest to Facebook.

ChapStick — which ironically urges people to "be heard at Facebook.com/ChapStick" — deleted negative comments en masse, which only made things worse. "The image isn't even that big of a deal — it's ChapStick's reaction to the criticism that galls," wrote Tim Nudd in an Adweek column headlined, "A Social Media Death Spiral." [9]

ChapStick's formal apology, issued six days after the flare-up began, gave critics new ammunition. The message referred to some of the comments it removed as spam, which it defined as "multiple posts from a person within a short period of time." This definition can also be applied to a vigorous conversation, so the crowd went wild again. "So, to those ChapStick fans whose comments were deleted — it was all your fault, you obnoxious, foul-mouthed, menacing spambots!" Nudd chided in *Adweek*.

The lesson: Have someone play the role of cynic and tell you how your statements can be used against you. Because your critics will do that if they can.

Don't expect to get air cover from the social network itself. Facebook's terms of service[10] are good at covering issues of intellectual property and privacy, but the social network stays away from First Amendment issues, libel and controversy. Its only relevant prohibitions in those areas are:

You will not bully, intimidate, or harass any user.

You will not post content that: is hateful, threatening, or pornographic; incites violence; or contains nudity or graphic or gratuitous violence.

You will not use Facebook to do anything unlawful, misleading, malicious, or discriminatory.

None of those prohibitions would have done Nestlé or ChapStick much good. When crises erupt in Facebook, it's because the situation *isn't* covered by standard disclaimers. With so little case study evidence to work from, communicators are pretty much making it up as they go along.

The best defense against an attack on your own Facebook page is to post a sub-page explaining your policies on appropriate content. Nestlé and Coca-Cola call this page "House Rules," and McDonald's labels it "Play Nice." In most cases, the language merely restates existing Facebook policies, but some brands press the rules a bit more.

For example, BP America's disclaimer says its Facebook presence is intended to "engage the public in an informative conversation about our efforts to meet growing energy demands around the world." It further reserves the right to delete content that is "obscene, indecent, profane, or vulgar … contain threats or personal attacks of any kind [or] are defamatory, libelous or contain ad hominem attacks."[11] That gives BP pretty wide latitude to regulate discussion, since the definition of "ad hominem" is so broad. BP had better be careful, though. If it defines the term too broadly, it risks making ChapStick's mistake of dismissing critics as spammers.

If you have to deal with a rebellion, treat everyone equally and don't edit selectively. Take a page from what Lowe's did in December 2011 when its Facebook page was swarmed over the retailer's decision to pull its ads from a reality show about ordinary Muslim families living in America. More than 9,000 comments were posted in 24 hours, many containing hateful language toward Muslims, and the attack generated widespread mainstream media coverage.

Lowe's chose to stay silent about the affair for a while, then it deleted the entire conversation and explained that the issue had gotten out of hand and that its Facebook page was not the appropriate place to discuss it. Fallout was minimal. Comments and media coverage were mostly favorable to Lowe's because the company didn't discriminate against any individual or group. It merely said the discussion should happen somewhere else.

The culture of Facebook assumes that conversation will be open and honest. If you approach Facebook expecting to control the conversation, be ready for trouble. If you're not ready to take a few arrows, then don't go there.

Hate Sites — Second Life from Search

Once a primary attack vector, hate sites have declined significantly in popularity as social networks have streamlined the process of building a destination and audience. Hate sites typically use a bastardized domain like USAirways-Sucks.com, GapSucks.org, IHateStarbucks.com and Iams-Cruelty.com, and feature news and forums that criticize the target company.

The problem with hate sites is that they require time and technical expertise to maintain, and their effectiveness depends upon search engine visibility and links from others. People who set them up often lose enthusiasm for the cause, leaving online ghost towns that haven't been updated in years. In contrast, Facebook comes with a lot of ready-made tools to build awareness, low administrative overhead and built-in community features. It isn't surprising that Facebook has displaced hate sites as a primary attack vector.

Because websites are more configurable than Facebook, some serve a purpose as a home base for campaigns whose principal activity has migrated to other platforms. An activist may post background documents, contact information, and press releases on a hate site and then take its active campaign to social networks.

Any company that's a candidate for attack should be sure to register variations of its domain that could potentially host hate sites. It's impossible to cover every base — the range of existing hate sites for just one airline include DeltaSucks, Delta'sTheWorst, NeverFlyDelta and DontFlyDelta — but the "IHate" prefix and "Sucks" suffix are obvious candidates.

Hate sites have one distinct advantage that can't be easily duplicated in other forums: search engine visibility. This can drive you crazy. A critical site that was abandoned years ago may show up on the first page of certain Google search results long after the original owners left town. Can you force hate sites off the front page of Google? Experts differ.

The issue of negative search engine optimization — sometimes called "Google bowling" — "is a highly debated question," said Mike Moran, co-author of *Search Engine Marketing, Inc.* "Some believe that it can work, and others don't."

The question is about how Google treats links from known spam sites or "link farms." These are clusters of websites set up by people who try to manipulate search engine results by creating a large number of essentially meaningless inbound links. Link quantity and quality are critical considerations in search rankings.

Search engines play a constant cat-and-mouse game with link spammers. They disregard links from known link farms, but new farms pop up every day, so it's hard for the search engines to keep up. We know that links from known link farms don't help a site's search visibility, but can they actually hurt? If so, then theoretically it would be possible to force a hate site down in search results by bombarding it with links from known link farms.

But Google isn't about to say whether that strategy would work. It doesn't want to give away any information to people trying to game the system. What we do know is that trying to elevate your own search visibility through link-farming is a losing game.

J.C. Penney was caught with its pants down in early 2011 when prominent search rankings for many of its domestic items drew the attention of SEO experts. It turned out that link farms were a critical factor, and Google promptly downgraded J.C. Penney by dozens of positions for many key terms. J.C. Penney maintained that it had no knowledge of the manipulation.[12]

Moran said the safer way to force detractors off the first page of search results "is to put out better content. It's actually easier than ever to move bad things out because newer content has more impact than ever before."[13]

Reddit — Explosive Potential

Have you ever heard of Reddit? We didn't think so. Social news sites have never been high on marketers' priority lists because of their reputation as being a playground for teen boys and nerds with few social skills. But that doesn't make them any less influential as news amplifiers.

Consider these numbers: 3.5 billion page views, 43 million unique visitors and more than 4,000 active communities in August, 2012, according to the site. Internet news sites saw a 64% increase in referral traffic from Reddit between June and July of that year.[14] Those statistics dramatize the amazing growth of this community that describes itself as "the front page of the Internet."

Reddit's star has risen as its predecessor, Digg, has faded. Both use a similar metaphor. Members submit links to pages, photos and videos they want to promote, and content rises and falls based upon votes by the members, or "redditors." There are 25 main communities — give or take — and more than 67,000 sub-communities.

Reddit's average member is a young male with some college education, and the site is particularly popular with techies.[15] There are very few rules, which makes Reddit a magnet for profanity, vulgarity and childish behavior. However, there's a lot of intelligent conversation that goes on there as well.

A particularly popular feature called "Ask Me Anything" allows anybody to promote their expertise, and celebrities, including Barack Obama, Jimmy Kimmel, Ron Paul and Stephen Colbert, have made guest appearances there to chat with members. On any given day, there are usually a couple of conversations going on with notable people.

To our knowledge, Reddit has not yet been a major contributor to a customer attack, but this site is growing fast and deserves attention. At its height in the early days of social media, Digg was capable of sending tens of thousands of visitors to a website in a matter of minutes. A negative customer story that hits the front page of Reddit can do the same. For now, redditors seem more interested in the cool and bizarre than in beating up on companies, but that could change.

Twitter — Attack Accelerant

"We've all heard that a million monkeys banging on a million typewriters will eventually reproduce the entire works of Shakespeare. Now, thanks to the Internet, we know this is not true."

Berkeley professor Robert Wilensky uttered that memorable quote in 1996. Were he speaking it today, he might refer instead to Twitter.

Twitter is the enigma of social networks. It's limited to text messages of 140 characters. It doesn't support photos, videos or applications natively. Instead of friends, it uses the simpler connection metaphor of follower or subscriber. Even its website is so weak that only a minority of its members use it.

How does a service with so little going for it create so damn much trouble?

The answer lies just above the number 3 on your keyboard. The hash tag (#), which was created by the Twitter community to help bring order to the service's inherent chaos, has become one of the Internet's most powerful organizing and amplification tools. It has helped Twitter become a core utility for arranging everything from book signings to mass protests. It has also established the popular microblog service as a prime channel for customer complaints and a favored tool of the critics we call "Casual Complainers." The #fail tag, which denotes poor performance by a person or company, is monitored by millions and is not one you want to see next to your name.

More than five years after Twitter launched, we still hear questions all the time about its value. To the uninitiated, it's a cacophony of voices sharing mostly useless information. And to a large extent that's true. The low barrier to entry and ease of use are two of Twitter's most endearing points. People can share anything, and they do. The power of Twitter comes from filtering out the junk and focusing on what's important to you.

Twitter's simplicity and accessibility are its strongest features. Messages can be sent and received on nearly any cell phone. Updates are instantaneous, which makes Twitter a valuable news tool. When seeking updates on a breaking news story, Twitter is often a much better source than the traditional media. Instead of relying on just one channel for information, you tap into the collective reports of many. Within a few seconds of news breaking anywhere, it's on Twitter. People with large Twitter followings can quickly magnify a complaint with a single re-tweet, and the media have learned to use Twitter both as an amplifier and a leading indicator of developing news.

While Twitter has occasionally been used to originate major attacks, its 140-character message limit doesn't permit much poetic license. Attackers are more likely to post their gripes on a blog or Facebook and use Twitter to extend their reach.

Twitter, Facebook, e-mail and other social networks are all amplifiers to some extent, but Twitter is unique in that its content is public. Facebook members share messages and links mainly with people they already know. In contrast, following a hash tag enables you to see all messages from all Twitter users about that topic. As a result, awareness can spread more quickly on Twitter than in any other social medium.

While the number of links shared on Twitter is less than one-third the number shared on Facebook, Twitter links are clicked on about 12% more often, according to a study by ShareThis, Starcom MediaVest Group and Rubinson Partners.[16] Sharing a tweet with one's followers is a two-click process on most PCs and mobile devices. This ease of sharing is why Twitter's amplification power is so great. About 40% of messages on Twitter include a URL. This makes Twitter a rapid vehicle for spreading long-form content such as videos and blog posts.

Another distinguishing — if not unique — value of Twitter is its speed. Messages can be fired off in a few seconds and instantly reach a global audience. The combination of speed and hash tags has made Twitter an effective medium for managing crowds. During the Occupy Wall Street protests in New York in 2011, for example, the #needsoftheoccupiers tag made it possible for supporters to identify and respond to requests from protesters for everything from books to pizza.[17] Organizers were able to move protests fluidly around the city by posting new locations to the #OWS tag.

Twitter has attracted an enthusiastic audience but not a very diverse one. The service is particularly popular with professional communicators, journalists, marketers, technology professionals and social media enthusiasts. Celebrities have embraced it as a way to connect directly with their fans (for example, more than 1,700 NFL players are on Twitter, according to Tweeting-Athletes.com), and media organizations have adopted it en masse to get bonus visibility for their coverage before it hits the newswires.

Acceptance by such visible people has perhaps made Twitter's influence disproportionate to its actual numbers. In fact, most Twitter members use the service very little. A 2009 study by Sysomos reported that 85% of Twitter users post less than one update per day, 21% have never posted anything and only 5% of Twitter users produce 75% of the content.[18]

However, even that small number can unleash an overwhelming amount of information. Dell Computer, for example, monitors about 25,000 messages per day in social media, most of them from Twitter, said Richard Binhammer, the former social media ambassador at Dell Computer. Dave Evans, author of *Social Media Marketing: An Hour a Day* and vice president of social strategy at Social Dynamx sums it up: "When you really stare down the Twitter firehouse and see what's coming at you, it's scary."

Bottom line: While Twitter may be small compared to Facebook, its vocal and influential member base can trigger a storm of controversy with amazing speed.

Twitter has played an amplification role in nearly every social media attack of the last four years. Journalists monitor trending hash tags to detect stories bubbling up through social media. Many create filtered tweet streams of the companies, government agencies and celebrities they cover. You should do the same for your company and brands.

Although major attacks rarely begin on Twitter, the service is a good way to identify problems before they get out of hand. One reason airlines watch Twitter so closely, for example, is that frustrated customers take first to their smart phones when delayed on the tarmac or frustrated at the ticket counter.

You've Been Hijacked

One unique form of Twitter attack is "brandjacking," or false accounts that appear to be real. The critic may use an account name that's substantially similar to a visible person or brand to post satirical or embarrassing messages.

The most notable example of Twitter brandjacking was @BPGlobalPR, which popped up during the 2010 oil spill in the Gulf of Mexico and began skewering BP as the company desperately struggled to stop the Deepwater Horizon disaster. The account attracted 160,000 followers — more than four times the following of BP's real North American Twitter account — and generated huge amounts of media coverage. The fact that the author remained anonymous until months after the crisis contributed to public curiosity.[19]

A rogue employee at publisher Condé Nast created an account that relayed bizarre comments overheard in the elevator. @CondeElevator was quickly shut down but not before its follower count exceeded 80,000. A similar account about elevator gossip at Goldman Sachs (@GSElevator) was still active and being followed by more than 260,000 people as of this writing. It's doubtful the investment banker would want its customers to hear comments such as "Retail investors should be circumspect of any offering they're able to get their hands on. If you can get it, you don't want it," but private conversations like that are now public record.

Twitter has cracked down on parody accounts that deliberately misrepresent a brand, but the policy doesn't apply to individuals, and variations of brand names are still allowed. Celebrities such as Hosni Mubarak, Roger Clemens and William Shatner have been portrayed by fake Twitter accounts, and brand variations such as @ATT_Fake_PR and @FakePewResearch provide satirical and often very funny send-ups of their targets. If you've been brandjacked you can appeal to Twitter directly, but be prepared to wait. If the satirist works within Twitter's guidelines, you have to take a more conventional crisis management approach.

The best defense against a Twitter attack is to listen. Free Twitter clients such as TweetDeck and HootSuite do a good job of catching mentions of your brand or products. If the volume of mentions is large, or if you want to filter for sentiment to detect a surge in negativity, you'll need a paid listening tool such as Radian6, Lithium or Sysomos.[20] Listening is easy and low-risk, but think twice before you let your branded Twitter account wade into a conversation. The precedent you set may come back to haunt you when people begin to expect a response. Unless you're prepared to devote resources to engaging on Twitter every day, the safest course is just to keep your ear to the ground.

We can't think of a good reason why every company today shouldn't have a branded Twitter account. Even if you use it only to disseminate press releases, it at least plants a flag in this increasingly critical community and it acclimates you to the culture and style of Twitter participants. Knowing who's influential can help you get messages to the right people in the event of a crisis.

Many consumer-focused companies now use Twitter for front-line customer support. Twitter can be a great tool for such purposes, but be aware of what you're getting into. When you set the precedent of addressing complaints within hours or minutes, customers will come to expect the same service all the time. Failing to deliver it can create a problem. Listen for a while to get an idea of the magnitude of the support task you'll face, then staff appropriately. Once you start proactively addressing customer complaints in public, it's very difficult to go back.

YouTube — Attack TV

Video has a unique power to spark emotion, as it has done in everything from natural disasters to political campaigns to the Occupy Wall Street movement. With video cameras embedded in nearly every cell phone that's sold today, any moment is now a potential media moment. For better or for worse.

The rapid rise of YouTube as a cultural phenomenon has been stunning. In early 2012, video uploads to YouTube hit 72 hours per *minute*,[21] a tenfold increase since 2007. As of this writing, YouTube was logging 4 billion video views per day and was the Web's number two search engine. With such vast reach, it's no surprise YouTube has also become a favored tool for attacking brands.

Some of the most notable YouTube attacks have used an organization's own collateral against it. The "Onslaught" TV ad produced by Unilever subsidiary Dove is a notable example. The 2007 ad chided the beauty industry for using images that taught young girls to equate self-esteem with physical appearance. It wasn't long before attack videos appeared that juxtaposed Onslaught with advertising for Unilever's Axe antiperspirant that featured scores of bikini-clad models.

Most people probably didn't know that Axe and Dove shared a corporate parent, and the spoof video, "A message from Unilever," ignited an unpleasant flurry of media criticism.[22] "Only one in 100 people may know that Unilever owns both brands," said Jim Nail, who was chief marketing officer for media-monitoring service

Cymfony at the time. "But that one person is likely to be participating in social media."

YouTube was the catalyst for 11 of 50 social media-inspired crises analyzed by Altimeter Group in a 2011 report. The attacks commonly take two basic forms:

Caught in the Act

These are embarrassing events captured by customers, usually on phone cameras, that demonstrate poor practices or customer service breakdowns. A 2007 video showing a dozen rats scurrying around a Greenwich Village Taco Bell embarrassed parent KFC and the New York Department of Health, which had passed the restaurant just a month earlier. KFC was forced to permanently close the store as well as nine others in New York City.

In December 2011, a U.S. resident's security camera captured a 20-second clip of a Federal Express delivery man unceremoniously throwing a computer monitor over a 5-foot iron fence instead of delivering it to the front door. The video was viewed more than 2.4 million times on YouTube within 24 hours, and FedEx was forced to swiftly post an apology video. If you search for UPS, FedEx and other home-delivery services on YouTube, you'll find lots of examples of drivers caught in traffic violations or mishandling customer deliveries.

There's not much you can do to anticipate or defend yourself against those kinds of attacks except to have a crisis plan in place. Companies that have large customer-facing organizations are the most vulnerable, and leaders need to realize that these days their customer service reps are potentially their weakest link. Any interaction with a customer is a potential video or audio clip. Both candidates in the 2008 presidential election were embarrassed by comments caught on cell-phone cameras, and political action committees now routinely employ stalkers to follow opposing candidates and to exploit every opportunity to catch them in a misstatement or lie.

Block that Comment!

There isn't much you can do when bloggers gang up on your business or products, but at least you can prevent the negativity from spilling over onto your own blog, right? Um, not really.

While corporate blogging has declined somewhat with the rise of alternative platforms, the fact remains that 23% of the Fortune 500 and 37% of the Inc. 500 still maintain public-facing blogs, according to the Center for Marketing Research at the University of Massachusetts at Dartmouth.[23] Many large companies have multiple blogs.

All blogging platforms support reader comments, although the feature can usually be turned off. Don't do that, though. Conversation is the essence of social media, and disabling comments turns a discussion into a monologue. You're better off having no blog at all, in fact, because restricting discussion makes you look clueless or arrogant. These days, critics simply take their gripes somewhere else.

It's better to post a "terms of service" statement in a separate page that outlines what you will and won't permit. Keep your list of prohibited content short and sensible: no offensive or hateful language, stalking, spamming, obscenity or intellectual property theft. We like the policy on General Motors' FastLane Blog.[24] It accepts the fact that dissent is part of an open discussion and it strives simply to keep the conversation civil.

We recommend against following the example set by Delta Airlines, whose user agreement runs to an incredible 6,600 words.[25] It's not surprising the Delta blog generates so little discussion. Anyone who would wade through such a ponderous legal document to post a comment would have to be very committed. Perhaps Delta's tome is a veiled message to critics to get lost.

The classic example of caught-in-the-act was the 2006 America Online incident we noted in the introduction. A recorded phone call of a customer service rep's overly aggressive efforts to retain a customer went viral and spread to national media in just five days.

AOL issued a formal statement saying the incident was an anomaly and that the rogue employee had been fired. It either didn't notice or ignored the fact that hundreds of people were lodging complaints about similar behavior in online forums. Then The Consumerist published an internal AOL document that proved that the rep's behavior was not only common but was actively encouraged by AOL management.

AOL shot itself in the foot. It had essentially sacrificed an employee for doing what he had been told to do, although perhaps a bit too enthusiastically. Its apology looked deceptive. No one was particularly surprised when AOL announced a few weeks later that it was getting out of the consumer Internet service provider business.

Spoofs

Sometimes a company's advertising messages can turn into parody videos that are meant to embarrass the firm or poke fun at its messages. These run the gamut from harmless to vicious, and responses must be tuned to avoid inflaming the situation further.

Spoofs can actually help boost brands, especially if they're creative and non-confrontational. Unilever has seen both sides of the issue. The "Onslaught" parodies cited earlier caught the company in an embarrassing double standard. However, an ad spot created in 2006 as part of the Dove Campaign for Real Beauty sparked several parody videos that enhanced the brand.

"Dove Evolution" depicted a rather plain-looking model being transformed into a billboard beauty thanks to makeup, professional photography and Photoshop. The ad, which was created exclusively for online presentation on a budget of only $135,000, has garnered over 15 million views on YouTube as of this writing and won several awards.

A professionally produced parody called "Slob Evolution" emerged not long thereafter. It shows a handsome young man being transformed into an overweight oaf using the same techniques as the original Dove video. It was nominated for several awards, including an Emmy, and has been viewed over 1.5 million times. Other knockoffs featuring an Asian subject, a drag queen and even a pumpkin have also appeared, driving over 5 million views and helping to spread awareness of the original Dove campaign.[26]

So, in the course of one year, Unilever experienced both the best and worst of what video parodies have to offer.

But not all parodies are so complimentary. Reports that the popular Chick-fil-A chain gave generously to anti-gay groups sparked a protest video in March 2012 that shows a trio of drag queens wallowing in sandwiches and waffle fries while singing, "Someday somebody's gonna make you want to gobble up a waffle fry. But don't go, don't you know Chick-fil-A says you're gonna make the baby Jesus cry." (It sounds better than it reads.)

The "Chow Down (at Chick-fil-A)"[27] spoof crossed over 1 million views in the first six weeks and seems destined to become a viral classic. It also presaged a much bigger controversy that erupted over Chick-fil-A's political leanings a few months later (see Chapter 10).

You need to walk a fine line when responding to spoof videos. One that doesn't push an agenda is probably harmless and may even be helpful. Cadbury Schweppes' innovative 2007 "Gorilla" campaign — which featured a character in a monkey suit drumming to Phil Collins' song "In The Air Tonight" — spawned many imitators with the company's tacit approval. "We feel that imitation is the most sincere form of flattery," a spokesman told the U.K.'s *Birmingham Mail.* "It's fine by us, and we will let it ride so long as it doesn't get out of hand."[28]

However, parodies that use a company's logo, theme music or advertising storyboard to its detriment can cross the line into brandjacking. That's next to impossible to combat because once a video is on the Internet, it quickly gets copied and reposted elsewhere. In 2010, Greenpeace created a gory parody of a Nestlé commercial for the Kit Kat candy bar showing an office worker biting into an orangutan's finger instead of a chocolate wafer. The video was a takeoff on an actual Kit Kat commercial and was intended to attack Nestlé's use of palm oil. Australia's *Daily Telegraph* but two years later copies were easy to find in several places, including on YouTube.

Chapter 7: Customer as Critic – the Power of Peer Reviews

Paul recently worked with a client that was the top-rated resort in its region on the TripAdvisor travel review site. Customer reviews drove so much business that the owner slashed his 2012 marketing budget by 60%. He didn't need to market; 80% of reservations came from online referrals. Customers were doing all the marketing he needed.

When Paul and his wife were in the market for carpeting, they chose a small local retailer that had racked up a string of rave reviews on Yelp, which is a prominent customer-review site for local businesses. The company's service lived up to its reputation. Paul asked how much impact Yelp had had on the retailer's business. "I'm embarrassed to tell you," the owner said. "It's been huge."

"Huge" was the same term Scott Wright used to describe the impact of travel review sites on the hospitality industry. Wright manages the Wyndham Wingate in Louisville, Ky., and he told us his company demands that he respond personally to any negative review posted on a major travel site within 72 hours. That doesn't mean just posting a comment; it means contacting the customer by phone. Wright isn't expected to satisfy every customer, but he does need to find out why they complained and make reasonable efforts to resolve the problem.

Customer reviews have become integrated into the fabric of many of our buying choices today, and their impact is transforming many industries. When we ask audiences, "Who has made travel choices in the last year based in part on online peer reviews?" 90% of the hands typically go up.

However, we believe that the travel and hospitality businesses are just the beginning. Consider Spiceworks, a thriving community for IT professionals on which members have posted thousands of reviews of everything from computer servers to computer consultants. "When I'm looking at a vendor, I don't Google it, I Spiceworks it," wrote one forum member.

At Glassdoor.com, employees rate the companies they work for, review executive performance and openly swap salary information. Imagine the impact on recruiting when company directories routinely include ratings by people who have worked there. All LinkedIn has to do is flick a switch to make that functionality real.

It's easy to forget what a torturous route peer-review services took to achieve this impact. In the late 1990s, trailblazing sites such as CitySearch and Epinions lacked the quality control features to prevent unscrupulous contributors from using them to either throttle their competition or pump their own products. Like early search engines, first-generation review sites became choked with so much spam that they were rendered effectively useless.

A lot has changed since then. While abuses still happen (as recently as late 2010, a group of U.K. hoteliers threatened to take TripAdvisor to court over allegedly spurious reviews), operators of crowdsourced opinion sites have learned to apply technology and peer pressure to thwart manipulators. This is now shaking some industries to the core. In the long term, we believe customer ratings will become part of the fabric of nearly every market, from blue jeans to jet airplanes.

Critical Mass

There are hundreds of customer review sites on the Internet, many of them in specialized niches. Travel is a particularly popular subject; TripAdvisor's parent company alone operates 17 travel brands.[1] Yelp has more than 70 million unique monthly viewers for its service, which rates local businesses.[2] Thumbtack and Angie's List rate local contractors. Kitchen Cabinet Reviews specializes in exactly what it says. And then there's Amazon, which has become one of the biggest publishers on the Web without actually publishing any of its own content. Reviews contributed by Amazon customers are a make-or-break factor in the success of products ranging from tablet computers to running shoes. We speak from experience when we say Amazon book reviews are now a critical factor in a book's success.

There is no one-size-fits-all formula for customer reviews, and their impact is situational. Products that have a high experiential component, such as restaurants, movies and books, are more heavily influenced by experienced reviewers who have acquired a reputation for quality work. Products that sell on features and specs, such as computers and cameras, tend to be influenced more by objective performance ratings and benchmarks. Products that combine elements of both, such as cars and stereo equipment, are affected by both factors.[3]

The Good, the Bad and the Ugly

First, let's address a common misperception. You may think you're immune from customer reviews because you never registered your business on the sites that publish them. The reality is that anyone can create a profile of your business on Yelp, TripAdvisor, Foursquare, Google+, Facebook and lots of other services without you even knowing it. They can list your address, phone number, operating hours and even post photos of your storefront without your permission. In most cases, you can get control of your profile by going through a simple verification process. However, the onus is on you to do that. Don't assume out of mind is out of view.

Reputable review sites have made great strides in addressing the quality issue. Yelp, which housed more than 30 million reviews of local merchants and services at the time of this writing, has worked with university researchers to develop programs that scrub content looking for keywords that indicate suspicious origins. Questionable reviews are moved to a sub-category that's visible but cordoned off and disclaimed.

Programmatic filtering is a complex and imperfect task, since the signposts often aren't obvious. Some of the warning signs of a fraudulent rating are downright bizarre. For example, reviews containing the word "husband" are more likely to be fake than those that don't, said Stephanie Ichinose, Yelp's Director of Communications.

Yelp actually errs on the side of caution. "We sacrifice content that looks suspicious in order to make sure reviews are helpful and trustworthy," Ichinose said. The company also discourages business owners from asking customers for favorable reviews on the theory that any attempts to game the system lower the quality of the product for everyone.

TripAdvisor's stated policy sounds simple: "We have a team of moderators that examine questionable reviews. We also use automated tools on the site that help flag questionable content for review, and our large and passionate community of millions of travelers keep [sic] an eye out on our site as well," reads a methodology statement on the popular website.

But it's clearly not that easy. TripAdvisor quality assurance professionals spend "thousands of hours every year ensuring the integrity of content," according to the company. "We also use automated tools that help flag questionable content for review." With more than 1,300 employees, quality control clearly doesn't come cheap.

Crowd Control

Nearly all review sites rely upon the wisdom of crowds for some measure of quality control. Some encourage visitors to rate content as helpful or flag it as suspicious. The latter usually prompts a look from a human arbiter. Reputable review sites such as Yelp and TripAdvisor require contributors to create a public profile of themselves that aggregates their activity and displays the ratings others have given them (pseudonyms are OK). Frequent contributors are rewarded with badges or titles such as TripAdvisor's "Senior Reviewer," which indicates they've crossed a threshold of respectability. With these signposts, most visitors can quickly figure out if a review comes from someone who knows what he or she is talking about.

Profiles are an essential element of reputable review sites, a kind of self-regulating quality control system. They hold reviewers accountable for published opinions, and reviews from anonymous or inactive profiles are assumed to be less credible by those who read them. On TripAdvisor, for example, the first reviews submitted by a new member are quarantined for a reality check by a staff member before being published. The audience is also encouraged to tag reviews for quality and helpfulness, with a point system elevating the work of the most-appreciated reviewers to a higher status. People who contribute the most value to the community are rewarded with recognition, followers, badges and exposure. It turns out that financial rewards are far less of a motivator than peer visibility.

Not all sites apply rigorous quality control measures, though. On Amazon, anyone can review anything as long as he or she has an account and has purchased something from the online retailer. The purchase doesn't even have to be the product being evaluated. Negative reviews can't be removed by anyone but the author. Amazon issues standard disclaimers about inappropriate language, paid placements and the like. The site relies upon its members to vet one another's work. The reviews deemed most useful by others rise to the top. The assumption is that the community will essentially police itself. And the system works pretty well.

Google+ (formerly Google Circles) takes a similar approach. Business owners can respond publicly to objectionable reviews, and there is a process for requesting inappropriate material to be removed. However, Google's philosophy is that honest give-and-take between businesses and their customers is a good thing. "We do not arbitrate disputes and more often than not, we leave the review up," its policy explains.

Structural Weaknesses

Despite all these quality control measures, online customer reviews have some inherent limitations that can't easily be solved by programmatic screen or reviewer rankings. As reviews have grown in importance, a cat and mouse game has developed between the operators of review sites and the people who try to manipulate them.

Technology research firm Gartner, Inc. expects about 15% of online reviews to be fake by 2014. One reason the problem is growing is that people have become comfortable with the quality of popular review services. "Customers feel that anything that is fake will already have been exposed," said Jenny Sussin, a Gartner senior research analyst, "but we know that even if a lot of people are getting caught, they'll just find different ways to do it."[4]

Amazon, in particular, has come under criticism for its hands-off approach to policing reviews, particularly in its books section. In 2012 *The New York Times* documented an underground economy of people who offer to write positive reviews for as little as $20 each. The newspaper quoted a data mining expert at the University of Illinois who estimated that about one-third of all consumer reviews on the Internet are fake.[5] *Forbes* noted that "carpet-bombing," or the seeding of review sites with a large number of negative ratings, has been used by some self-published authors to undermine buyers' confidence in positive reviews of competing titles. The lack of laws to prevent such malicious behavior means that "there are huge benefits to behaving unethically but very little cost for those caught doing so." [6]

Writing in *Scientific American*, Michael Moyer concluded, "The wisdom of crowds may neither be wise nor necessarily made by a crowd. Its judgments are inaccurate at best, fraudulent at worst."[7]

Moyer quoted Wharton professor Eric K. Clemons, citing numerous inherent biases in all consumer review systems:

- People who write reviews have already purchased the product and are therefore inclined to be favorably disposed toward it.

- People tend to review products they love or hate but not those that inspire apathy. "These feelings lead to a lot of one- and five-star reviews of the same product," Moyer wrote.

- Only a small number of people ever write online reviews, which means they have disproportionate influence over ratings. "What appears to be a wise crowd is just an oligarchy of the enthusiastic," he remarked.

The last point is a characteristic of all online communities that is sometimes referred to as the 90:9:1 rule. That means 1% of community members participate actively, 9% participate occasionally and 90% never participate at all. However, an oligarchy of the enthusiastic doesn't necessarily demean the value of what they say. If you scan the ratings dispersion of frequent Yelp contributors, for example, you'll see about a 3:1 ratio of favorable to unfavorable reviews. That probably reflects the experiences most of us have with the companies with which we do business. Most are pretty good, and a few are awful. The Yelpers we spoke to said they never trash a company online unless they're convinced it deserves it.

Sam Decker, the founding chief marketing officer at Bazaarvoice, bristled at Moyer's "fraudulent" comment. "Only a very small minority of reputable companies would officially sanction fraudulent reviews," he said. "At Bazaarvoice, we saw only a fraction of a percent of reviews that even *could* be fraudulent."

Money for Nothing, Marketing for Free

Well-run businesses that are committed to customer satisfaction can enjoy a gusher of business from customer endorsements, but making it to the top of the ratings heap hardly gives a business permission to coast.

The Mandarin Oriental is the top-rated hotel in Atlanta on TripAdvisor with more than 250 reviews as of this writing, nearly all of them glowing. The endorsements have enabled the Mandarin to maintain its premium prices and cut its acquisition costs, but it also has the staff hopping to keep its coveted top position. "Social media is vital to our business today," said Micarl Hill, the hotel's managing director. "But it also keeps us on our toes. People can tell everybody about a bad stay with the push of a button. What they say isn't always fair, but we take it seriously." In other words, a top rating puts *more* pressure on a business to perform than a bunch of middling reviews because the payoff of reaching the top – and the risk of falling from that position – is so high.

Review sites are rarely a factor in grassroots customer attacks. Trusted members of the community are less likely to have short-term agendas or to jeopardize their elite status by ganging up on brands or promoting agendas. One-time critics are flagged programmatically or dismissed by visitors because they don't have a reputation. Credible review sites use Captcha codes or e-mail confirmations to keep spammers out. Any effective effort to flood the community would require a lot of thought and investment.

That doesn't mean customers don't sometimes use reviews to make a statement. Users of Skitch, a screenshot utility for the iPhone, were enraged when Evernote acquired the developer and released a new version of the software that many people thought was inferior to its predecessor. Critics showed their displeasure by trashing the upgrade on the iTunes stores, slicing its 4.5-star overall rating to 1.5 stars in just a couple of weeks. Few customers are as passionate as iPhone enthusiasts, though.

Perhaps the biggest risk of customer review sites is to small businesses that don't generate a lot of online feedback or that are in niche categories such as landscaping or dentistry. A merchant with only two reviews can look bad if both are negative, but site operators say visitors tend to naturally discount such evaluations. It's unlikely that a small number of dissatisfied customers are mounting an attack. More often they just had a bad experience, and a call or e-mail can resolve the situation.

What to Do About Bad Reviews

Some services let you subscribe to reviews, so you should arrange for a notification to be sent to you from the site itself, just in case Google Alerts has a bad day. Accept glowing reviews with quiet pride. If you send thank-you notes or rewards, send them to everybody and don't single out reviewers because that could be construed as manipulative. Also, don't openly encourage customers to write reviews lest you run afoul of site policies.

When people flame you, act with deliberate speed. If it's clear who the critics are, contact them directly, thank them for their feedback and find out what went wrong. If you don't know who the reviewer is, most sites provide a way to contact people through anonymous e-mail. The best antidote to a bad review is to speak to the customer directly. Most people are so flattered by the attention that they amend or take down the review. We asked many business owners about the palliative effect of direct contact with aggrieved customers, and the consensus is that 80% to 90% of complaints can be satisfied with a simple phone call. A small giveback or discount on a future visit is a good idea, but restrain your generosity. You don't want to look like you're trying to buy people off.

If you can't contact a complainer or reach a reasonable resolution, post a response to the review explaining your side of the story. Note that you made a good faith effort to address the problem, and be sure to restate your commitment to customer satisfaction. Never attack the reviewer, although it's fine to address factual mistakes or explain mitigating circumstances like an illness that left you short-staffed. You'll get brownie points just for making the effort.

Silence is golden in some cases, particularly if the complainers are the "C.A.V.E. people" referred to in Chapter 5. You're not going to get very far trying to please them.

"Some people wake with the desire to ruin someone else's day," wrote Lisa Barone of Outspoken Media. "Trying to engage said miserable person will only incite a war and will likely become far more damaging. If the comment isn't outrageous or slanderous on its own, there's no need to get it more attention."[8]

Silence in the face of growing unrest is a lousy strategy, though. At best you'll look out of touch, and persistent silence may be perceived as arrogance. Barone says you should monitor a negative thread for evidence of momentum. If that happens, "handle it at its source ... get in the conversation and help calm it down. Often, a few words from you will be enough to soothe the hype and get the conversation back on track."

If most of your reviews are glowingly positive, take advantage of all the features the site offers to burnish your presence. Fill out your profile as completely as possible, including links to appropriate areas of your website. Post photos of your happy employees. Take

Four Out of Five Customers Recommend

We hear a lot of questions about the integrity of online review sites, most of them tinged with anxiety. "Restaurant owners don't really have a kind word to say about Yelp," says Michael Atkinson, CEO of FohBoh.com, a social network for restaurant professionals. That's strange, because more businesses benefit from crowdsourced reviews than suffer from them.

User ratings work particularly well for the little guy who has to compete against big brands and big ad budgets. Numerous studies have verified that people are more likely to share positive experiences than negative ones, and even lousy reviews can have an upside.

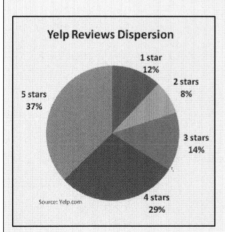

An early 2012 survey of 1,481 U.S. consumers by Chadwick Martin Bailey found that the top two reasons people complete satisfaction surveys are "to share a good experience" (57%) and "to improve the company" (50%). While more than 80% of the respondents had posted at least one negative review, only 35% said their principal reason for completing satisfaction surveys was to register negative opinions.[9] Yelp publishes a quarterly summary of the dispersion of all new reviews across its one- to five-star spectrum, and the pros outnumber the cons by about a factor of three.

Customer reviews tend to benefit small businesses disproportionately because they call attention to unique experiences. A 2011 research report by Harvard Business School assistant professor Michael Luca analyzed more than 60,000 reviews of restaurants in the Seattle area and concluded that each additional star in a quality rating equated to 5% to 9% in increased business.[10] In other words, an eatery with a five-star rating could expect to do 10% to 20% more business than a comparable one with three stars. Interestingly, Luca's formula worked only for locally owned establishments. Franchises such as TGI Friday's and Olive Garden Italian Restaurants were statistically unaffected by customers reviews, perhaps because customers expect consistent quality and are less likely to be strongly influenced by a single visit.

We contacted several of the most prolific reviewers on Yelp to ask what motivates them to contribute so much and what criteria matter to their own ratings. With an average of more than 1,500 published reviews each, these people define Clemons' "oligarchy of the enthusiastic." We found them to be a pretty upbeat group.

"I enjoy giving great positive feedback for a business and very few of my reviews are negative," said Michelle Colombo, who has filed nearly 1,300 reviews under the name "Wine Goddess." "I have found many places I never would have known about if it weren't for Yelp. My favorite part has been meeting so many like-minded friends."

"I look at Yelp as a great way to talk about cool places, and I've always believed in supporting local merchants," said Nish Nadaraja, a San Franciscan who has filed nearly 1,800 reviews. Asked if he prefers to use Yelp to reward or punish businesses, he responded, "Definitely reward. I intentionally hold back from writing negative reviews until I've visited an establishment at least a couple of times, and even then I try to give context for my experience." His track record supports that philosophy: nearly 85% of his reviews are either four or five stars.

"For me, the excitement is discovering the really great eats. I prefer to give positive reviews, and thus I probably have a bias toward heaping more praise on businesses that are great," wrote Rob C. of Palo Alto, Calif., who declined to give his full name. "Offer the best product at the best price with a smile, and you'll please the majority." That said, the author of more than 2,700 Yelp reviews also gives out a lot of three-star ratings and knows what he doesn't like. "The biggest mistake is when businesses act like a touristy place, meaning that they don't care about getting the repeat customer," he said.

Even poor reviews have an upside. Customers who take the time to express an opinion care enough about their experience to share, which means they probably care enough to give the business another chance. Since most unhappy customers leave without saying why, these detractors are valuable candidates for rescue. Don't squander the opportunity.

advantage of the widgets many operators provide that let you advertise your top-rated status on your own website. Some will even give you stickers to paste on your storefront window.

Customer review sites tend to punish businesses that deliver extraordinarily poor experiences and shower reward on those that go the extra mile. If you are middle of the road, they probably won't make much difference. How much attention you pay to them depends on how much perceived benefit you get.

Should You Host Customer Reviews?

Most big Internet retailers host consumer reviews on their sites as a convenience to shoppers, but brands that make the products those retailers sell have been much more reluctant about subjecting their wares to the wisdom of crowds. The resistance is understandable: Why would you want customers complaining about the stuff you make in your own online store?

The surprising truth is that customer reviews — even negative ones — are good for business. While individual products may suffer, the latitude that hosted reviews gives companies to address problems and correct misconceptions more than makes up for lost sales of products that probably weren't very good anyway.

Computer printer maker Epson compared a month's worth of visitor activity after launching reviews on its branded site in 2010 and found that shoppers who read reviews showed higher intent to purchase, higher conversion, and greater revenue per visitor than shoppers who didn't.[11] Epson calculated that review readers spent 98% more on average than non-readers.

Online retailer AlpacaDirect.com, which sells clothing made from alpaca fur, replaced a page of cherry-picked customer testimonials with a customer review engine and saw sales jump 23% on reviewed items. Sales even grew for products that got negative comments, such as a golf cardigan that was described as "kinda sweaty" and a "poor fit."[12]

There are compelling reasons to let customers spout off in your own space:

- A company that hosts customer reviews has at least some latitude to manage the process and to respond directly to detractors, which means negative reviews can more easily be reversed.

- People are more likely to share positive experiences than negative ones, so a company that is confident in its products and people probably has little to fear.

- A little negativity isn't necessarily bad. The occasional one-star review validates the integrity of the entire feedback program.

- Trust is more essential to customer loyalty than ever, and feedback mechanisms are evidence that a company can be trusted.

There are practical benefits, too. A product that receives many negative reviews probably needs to be fixed or should be dropped from inventory. It's faster to discover stinkers from immediate customer feedback than by waiting for the quarterly sales report.

More important, though, is that positive reviews give prospective buyers validation for their decisions. That first impression is increasingly important in a hurried-up world in which people have less time to consider options. A 2012 survey of 427 U.S. consumers by ClickFox found that nearly half cited first impressions as the most critical time to gain their loyalty, and 10% said loyalty is formed before they even decide to do business with a company.[13]

"The mere presence of a mix of positive and negative feedback is seen as more authentic and builds trust," wrote Erin Nelson, former CMO of Dell Computer and current CMO of feedback-management firm Bazaarvoice, in AdAge Digital. "It proves to customers that you value their voices and embrace transparency...[A]uthentic customer feedback about a product or service, whether positive or negative, improves conversion when compared to having none available."[14]

Hate Me, Please!

Brand-hosted reviews may even compensate for negative feedback on independent sites. While we were researching this chapter, we came across a published case study of Teleflora's success with on-site customer reviews of its bouquets and flower arrangements.[15] Indeed, Teleflora's site is packed with four- and five-star reviews. Strangely, that isn't the case outside of the Teleflora cocoon.

The company had a dismal .6-out-of-10 rating on TrustPilot and a "Terrible" rating on Customer Service Scoreboard. Ripoff Report listed 39 complaints, and The Consumerist documented numerous problems with the company's Valentine's Day service.

Why the disparity? Former Bazaarvoice CMO Sam Decker's theory is, "People review Teleflora's *customer service* on external sites, whereas the reviews on Teleflora's site are about specific *products."* Data collected over a seven-year period by Bazaarvoice shows that reviews on branded sites average of 4.3 out of five, whereas the average on independent sites is lower. "When you share a review about service, it's *their* fault, whereas when you share a negative product review it's *my* fault for buying it," he said.

Bazaarvoice spokesman Mickey Nelson suggested that the nature of the product affects review dispersion. He pointed to a post on the company's blog that concluded, "We see higher five-star ratios in product categories that are strongly associated with positive feelings and experiences. Flowers/Gifts have the highest (75%), followed by jewelry (70%) and pets (68.6%). Think about it — we associate many of these [purchases] with emotionally satisfying moments, like weddings, birthdays, and anniversaries."[16]

Negative reviews can actually increase sales of little-known products by raising brand awareness. Researchers from Stanford University and the Wharton School of Business analyzed sales of 250 books reviewed in *The New York Times*. They found that bad reviews of established authors triggered average declines of 15%, but negative reviews of *little-known* authors actually drove sales up by an average of 45%. After one *Times* reviewer cited "many flaws" in Dirk Wittenborn's *Fierce People*, sales more than quadrupled.

"By making consumers aware of a book they would otherwise not know about, even the harshest review can be a boon," wrote Wharton's Jonah Berger.[17]

The rise of social networks has added a new and appealing dynamic. Companies can now make it easy for reviewers to share their opinions in their social networks with a single click of a "share" button. The same dynamics that boost participation in social networks, such as peer recognition and leader boards, can also benefit brands.

Athletic shoemaker Skechers features more than 60,000 product reviews on its site as of this writing. In 2012, it introduced the Skechers Elite program to reward customers with points for submitting reviews and answering questions about its products. Points can be redeemed for discounts and free shoes. The program was prompted by data that showed that visitors who asked a question on the website and received an e-mail response were 32% more likely to become customers. By enlisting other customers in the process, Skechers hopes to speed responses and boost conversion rates.

Nevertheless, not every company benefits from hosting its own reviews. Airlines and restaurants, for example, basically sell one product. It wouldn't make sense to ask customers to evaluate individual routes or menu items. The transparency that reviews demand also means being prepared for the consequences. A cultural commitment to customer satisfaction is essential.

Chapter 8: Mainstream Media – Enabler or Enforcer?

Joe Weisenthal is the lead financial blogger at Business Insider. He routinely works from 4 a.m. until 9 p.m. in a caffeine-induced frenzy that often results in more than 150 tweets and 15 blog posts in a day. "Some of what he writes is air and sugar. Some of it is wrong or incomplete or misleading. But he delivers jolts of sharp, original insight often enough to hold the attention of a high-powered audience," said a *New York Times* profile.[1] Joe Weisenthal is a superstar of new media.

Business Insider is a successful online news service that has been rated a top financial news site by some of the most influential media brands in the U.S. But you've never seen financial news like this. Headlines such as "14 Common Ways People Cheat At Golf" and "Everything You Ever Wanted To Know About Russian Mail Order Brides" adorn the home page. Cheesecake photos of models in bikinis run adjacent to statistics about the Greek financial crisis. It's *The Wall Street Journal* meets *Weekly World News*, but it has 15 million monthly visitors and it's turning a profit.

There are many burgeoning online publications like Business Insider. One of them is The Huffington Post, which came out of nowhere to become one of the top news sources on the Web in just five years and sold to AOL for $315 million. The site employs a staff of editors, but the volume of submissions from contributors is so overwhelming that fact-checking is left mainly to the writers.

The Huffington Post publishes submission guidelines that urge contributors to verify facts, but it ultimately admits that "edits are overwhelmingly small."[2] Compare that to the *The Washington Post*, which in its heyday subjected front-page news stories to as many as a dozen editing cycles. Traditionalists may cringe at such shortcutting of the rules, but The Huffington Post won a 2012 Pulitzer Prize in National Reporting.

Cringe-worthy

Many veteran communicators regard the new crop of online news sources with a mixture of fear and disgust. There is so much bad information on the Internet that it often seems nothing is believable anymore. Devastating cutbacks in staff and budgets at even the most reputable publications have made fact-checking an expensive luxury. Bloggers don't abide by long-respected journalistic standards such as triple-checking critical facts, and competition from citizen journalists and new media outlets has put pressure on even the biggest brands to put speed ahead of accuracy.

"When news is unfolding in real time, it's a matter of seconds to be at the top of Google search results," says Jeremiah Owyang, industry analyst at Altimeter Group.

Critics have reason for concern, but the new reality is that in the hypertensive world of online news, where only minutes separate scoop from also-ran, attention to detail is an expensive luxury.

In 2008, TechCrunch's Erick Schonfeld wrote that the popular blog's philosophy was that it's better to post an incomplete story quickly than to wait until all the facts are known.[3] The Consumerist, which is one of the most respected consumer advocacy blogs, did almost no fact-checking during its early years. Its content consisted primarily of e-mail submissions that were lightly edited before publication. Ben Popken, who served as editor-in-chief for nearly six years, had no formal journalism training and had worked as a delivery man not long before joining Consumerist. He got the job because the previous editor's mother read his blog.[4]

A *Columbia Journalism Review* survey of 665 consumer magazines in 2010 found online content wasn't fact-checked or copy-edited as rigorously as printed content.[5] Nearly half the respondents to the survey said their copy-editing standards are lower for online content than for print, and 11% didn't copyedit online material at all.

121

More than one-quarter of the respondents also said they're less careful about fact-checking the information they publish online. *CJR* researchers attributed the disconnect between print and online quality control to the primacy of speed in the digital publishing world.

This makes purists cringe. It's as if the gentlemanly craft of journalism that had been honed over the past three centuries took a huge step backward around 2004. These concerns are understandable, but they fail to take the unique characteristics of new media into account. They also overlook history.

A Distant Mirror

Our assumptions about journalistic quality are actually rooted in relatively recent developments. In the earliest days of newspapering, publishers were people who had the money to use the press to promote an agenda. Salacious stories were routinely published for the purpose of selling papers. Every title produced by these "pamphleteers" had something to sell.[6] Fact and opinion were jumbled together, and attribution was practically unknown. Publishing flourished; the city of Philadelphia had more than 70 newspapers during the 18th century.

Those early publishers had a lot in common with today's bloggers. Empowered by cheap access to publishing technology, people seized the opportunity to find an audience for their opinions and to influence markets and institutions. Readers understood this, and they learned to triangulate fact from multiple sources. Impartial journalism was unknown to the founding fathers. When they wrote the First Amendment, the journalism they sought to protect was similar to that practiced by bloggers today.

The free-for-all continued well into the 20th century. Prior to the introduction of television, rumors and innuendo were often reported as fact. Legendary publishers such as Joseph Pulitzer and William Randolph Hearst backed political candidates whom they promoted through their reporting. News was often as much entertainment as it was information.[7] Gossip and story-telling sold newspapers, though, which enabled the successful titles to invest in quality. The seeds of the Pulitzer Prize-winning journalism we respect today were planted by the pre-World War II version of top 10 lists.

Social media is back to the future. Now that low-cost publishing tools can make anyone a journalist, the rules of engagement are being reset, but with one big difference: Online publishing assumes that publishing isn't permanent. It's easier to rationalize speculation if you know that mistakes can be quickly corrected. That isn't the case in traditional print and broadcast.

Let's take Wikipedia as an example. It's constantly changing, and false information is posted every day. However, mistakes don't live long because an army of volunteer fact-checkers quickly corrects them. Wikipedia is a self-healing information source. Although some people doubt its validity, research has consistently documented that Wikipedia is at least as accurate as traditional printed encyclopedias.[8]

New-media journalists care little about the traditional standards of their profession. Time doesn't permit them to check everything they report. They gather content from multiple online sources and validate by triangulation, much as readers of 18th-century newspapers did. If the same information is being reported by several trusted sources that aren't citing one another, then it's assumed to be true. Business Insider's Weisenthal rarely uses the phone, according to the *Times* profile. He gets most of his information from blogs, tweets and other items posted in social channels. The Huffington Post's contributor guidelines urge writers to link to their source material as validation rather than making phone calls. In these ways, time-tested journalism standards are being rewritten.

"I don't know how to write an inverted pyramid story or even really what that is. I do know how to write for different platforms, be scrappy and break news. I've had zero important alum connections and never got an internship at a big daily. And, in hindsight, that's probably the greatest stroke of luck I could have had," wrote Sarah Lacy on TechCrunch.[9] Lacy is considered a superstar of new media. A former columnist at *BusinessWeek*, she spreads her journalism across multiple blogs, online video shows and contributions to top publications. The title of her second book sums up the style of the successful new-media journalist: "Brilliant, Crazy, Cocky."

What does this have to do with a book about customer attacks? We think plenty. One of the challenges of managing reputation in today's chaotic media world is to understand how people determine what is true. That was pretty easy to do in the days of media monoliths, but today's media are so fragmented that trust is fragile. We need sites like Snopes.com, FactCheck.org and The Straight Dope to help.

Media Disruption

We'll resist the temptation to slam mainstream media for failing to see years ago that its business model was so vulnerable. That song has been sung to death. Suffice to say that the high-yield advertising business that delivered reliable 10% after-tax margins and supported large staffs of professional journalists has gone the way of the horse and buggy. Layoffs have reduced editorial staffs at many newspapers by 40% or more, and local TV stations have replaced experienced (and expensive) senior journalists with cheaper junior reporters and interns. Don't believe us? Watch your local evening news.

That doesn't mean traditional media aren't relevant. On the contrary, the media's influence is arguably stronger today than ever. The Newspaper Association of America has reported that readership of newspaper content in print and online is at an all-time high, even as the business model implodes. In a democratized information world, people rely more than ever on trusted sources to tell them what's true. Read any account of a viral marketing success or disaster, and you'll see that the turning point was when newspapers and TV stations picked up on the story. The problem is that competitive pressure and cost cuts at those organizations have forced them to sacrifice their most important asset: quality.[10]

Newsroom employment at U.S. newspapers declined about 25% between 2006 and 2009, according to the American Society of Newspaper Editors. It continues to fall steadily. At the same time, staff workloads have increased. Many newspaper reporters who were once expected to file a single 750-word story a day now produce three and four times as much copy to compensate for depleted staffs, while also being pressed to blog and tweet their works in progress. Many are asked to produce video and audio content as well. It's perhaps not surprising that two media jobs made Career-Cast's list of the 10 worst jobs for the first time in 2012: newspaper reporter and broadcaster.[11]

Moreover, the competitive landscape has changed. Online news sites such as TMZ and The Politico trade on their ability to be first with a story. Many are willing to go with sketchy information on the assumption that errors can always be corrected with minimal impact. The competitive pressure is greater than ever, and even the best journalists are understandably tempted to cut corners. The news media's traditional discipline of corroborating information is increasingly a crap shoot.

In short, mainstream media institutions today are unpredictable giants. Their power to amplify is still formidable, but their ability to perform due diligence has been hobbled. They are particularly susceptible to the media-savvy attacker who's more than happy to do the grunt work.

New News Dynamic

Most online customer attacks follow similar trajectories. A complaint starts with an individual's experience or isolated news report. Customers begin to share and interpret the news through social channels such as Twitter and Facebook. Bloggers catch on and aggregate the commentary into a trend. The conversation may reach amplifiers that elevate this attention, like Twitter's trending hash tags or the home page of Reddit.

The media monitor all of these channels. Social media has rapidly become a prime information source for journalists. According to a 2011 survey of journalists by the Society of New Communications Research and Middleberg Communications:

- 75% use Facebook as a tool to assist in reporting;

- 69% use Twitter;

- 68% believe reliance on social media has increased significantly;

- 95% believe social media can be a reliable tool for sourcing stories;

- 69% use mobile technology to search, use social networking apps and capture videos and pictures for reporting.[12]

Mainstream media have a special role in validating the newsworthiness of an attack. Large corporations in particular know that a certain amount of grumbling is part of the background noise of customer conversations, but that doesn't mean every complaint is a crisis. The trick is to know when the story has jumped the track because once it does, it can spread like kudzu.

Customer attack stories are ready-made media fodder. The complaints are laid out clearly in writing, and background is easy to find through search and discussion threads. The leaders of an attack usually identify themselves and are easy to contact. Most are more than willing to speak to the media, and other participants can be rounded up by simply posting inquiries in social networks.

"The media love the story of David vs. Goliath, and these stories resonate in social," said Jeremiah Owyang, the Altimeter Group analyst. "The media have been trained that these are great stories. They're easy to pluck off the wire, and you don't have to do any research. You don't need to interview anybody. It's all there."

Commercial blogs are an effective attack vector because of their insatiable need for content to fill their bottomless news holes. Savvy publicists are learning to use blogs as a channel to reach big-brand media. Controversial media strategist Ryan Holiday, author of *Trust Me, I'm Lying: Confessions of a Media Manipulator*, explained this strategy in an interview with Mixergy.com:

> *These are bloggers, but at the end of the day, they want to be cutting-edge real journalists...*

I sent an anonymous tip from a fake e-mail address ... to two different blogs who both independently picked it up. [S]hortly thereafter [it] got picked up by the Village Voice, and what I realized very early on was, where do reporters get the news? They get the news from blogs. It's not like reporters are out there pounding the pavement, looking for news or overhearing gossip. They read blogs, and so I found a very clear link between small blogs and medium-sized blogs to big blogs, and then [to] the national press.[13]

Customer attacks are the conflicts media love: powerless consumer pitted against ruthless corporate giant. The little guy is by default the object of sympathy, and the big company can't be trusted.

Local television stations are particularly vulnerable to manipulation because the story makes great theatre and junior reporters lack the skepticism of the veterans they replaced. The "victims" in these stories are often local residents who are easy to capture on camera in their humble homes with the worn-out furniture and paint peeling from the walls. The corporate antagonist may be portrayed simply as a logo or an office building. Corporate spokesmen deliver emotionless statements. Corporations are terrible about humanizing their public image, which is why we encourage you to bring your likeable spokespeople out from behind the logo. Media relations is becoming a lot more personal.

When it comes to customer attacks, the media tend to play follow the leader. Google any of the case studies mentioned in this book, and you'll see what we mean. As long as a story stays local or remains the exclusive domain of bloggers, things probably won't get out of hand. When it jumps to *USA Today, The Wall Street Journal* or even New York's *Daily News*, however, it's going to spread far and wide. This can create a short-term storm of media activity, but the effects are rarely long-lasting. The good news is that customer attacks rarely generate much long-term media interest, compared to, say, the indiscretions of a political candidate. Business stories don't have much mainstream appeal to begin with, and attacks can usually be contained with a sound response.

This is the new world of U.S. media as we see it. Few corporate communications executives will criticize media on the record; however, Procter & Gamble's Paul Fox is an exception. Speaking about the Pampers crisis described in Chapter 1, he said, "Certain elements of the media paid very little attention to the facts. Even a cursory examination of that Facebook page would have revealed activities that should have set off alarm bells that this wasn't as straightforward as it might look. But if you had an angry parent, a crying baby and large corporation, you've got a story.

"Many local television stations had got what they wanted," Fox continued, "an interview with an angry mom complemented by comments lifted from a Facebook site and visuals showing a crying baby and a Pampers logo. All that was left was to try to get a comment from Pampers. It was a relatively easy story for them to cover. In those cases, you need to ensure that the brand understands that the coverage is going to be negative and to focus on getting its message through other channels."

In Chapter 10, we outline steps communicators can take to avoid this vicious cycle. The good news is that victims can use the same tools and channels as their attackers to correct misinformation. Communicators who are well-wired into the ecosystem of their industry's influencers can disseminate information from the bottom up as well as from the top down, as Scott Monty did in The Ranger Station case described in Chapter 3. Most corporate communicators aren't so plugged in to the new cycle of influence, however. That will come with time — and more attacks.

Ultimately, media gravitate toward the truth, and the faster an organization under attack discloses everything it knows about the situation, the quicker the crisis subsides. "A well-managed crisis gets all the bad news over with up front by aggressively dealing with the problem, and the volume drops precipitously after the first week. The fallout from a poorly handled crisis can drag on for months," noted measurement expert Katie Paine.[14]

Paine cited Levi Strauss and Columbia/HCA Healthcare as examples of how to manage and *not* manage a problem. When Levi's announced its first-ever layoffs in 1998, it took steps to lessen the pain by also announcing grants to the communities affected by job loss. Negative coverage dissipated within two weeks. In contrast,

Columbia denied rumors of business problems for months before announcing lower financial results. Once the facts came out, the backlash drove the company to replace much of its top management. Both of those stories happened before social media was a factor. Today, the volume and speed of coverage would be amplified by orders of magnitude.

Even a debunked story doesn't necessarily die these days. It can live for years in search engine results, and social media creates a soapbox for people who have the will and energy to perpetuate it. As of this writing, the Pampers Dry Max case had been effectively closed for more than two years, yet new comments continued to appear every week or two on the "Bring back the OLD CRUISERS/SWADDLERS" Facebook page. DuPont long ago put to rest rumors that Teflon causes cancer, but questions about the 20-year-old myth still pop up regularly in online discussions. Misinformation flourishes in the echo chamber of cynics and conspiracy theorists, and that is a consequence of democratized media that we will have to live with.

Your objective shouldn't be to quash bad news entirely, just as you shouldn't strive to delight every single customer. Get the story out of mainstream media, reduce noise to a manageable level and keep the bad news off the first page of Google results. That means having good listening tools, strong influencer relations and a tested and reliable crisis plan. We'll deal with those strategies next.

Chapter 9: An Ounce of Prevention

Up until now we've mostly talked about the causes, motivations, tools and tactics of customer attacks, but what you really want to know is how to avoid them, or at least be prepared when they occur. Well, thanks for bearing with us because it's time to get to the point.

There have been lots of great books written about crisis communications, so we won't rewrite them here. We'll recap a few basics, but our main interest is to show you how to use the same social media tools attackers use in your own defense. That doesn't mean fighting a multi-front, head-exploding battle across every online community out there. What you really want to do is drive the conversation back to a place you control. It's just that you don't often have much choice where engagement begins.

Managing through an attack is all about prevention, planning and knowing what role each person plays in the process. It all starts with listening to your market and understanding who influences your stakeholders. We'll take each topic in turn.

Learn to Listen

The best crisis scenario is one that never occurs, and that's where listening is vital. We assume you already have some basic listening tools in place, such as customer satisfaction surveys, feedback forms and focus groups. Those tools all have value, but they can now be complemented by a vast array of technologies that tap into online conversations.

These range from simple Google Alerts to high-end packages such as Nielsen BuzzMetrics, which can cost thousands of dollars per month. Many of our clients use Salesforce.com's Radian6 or Sysomos, which are both moderately priced and do a good job of listening to conversations in public places such as Twitter and blogs.[1]

Tools are only part of the equation, though, and there are limits to what automation can do. Big brands may be mentioned tens of thousands of times a day on Twitter and Facebook alone. Only a few of these mentions may be actionable, and it takes a combination of filters and human respondents to identify them.

Then there are brands whose names are common terms that people use in many different contexts (like Crest or Mars), mean something else in other languages (Milano) or both (Viva). Finally, there's sentiment analysis, which is the devilishly difficult problem of trying to figure out whether references are positive, negative or neutral. Many tools attempt to analyze sentiment, but even the best ones make plenty of mistakes.

When monitoring Twitter specifically, look for these signs of a developing attack:

- Trending hash tags that include your company name (most Twitter clients display the top trending tags by default; WhatTheTrend.com can give you more detail);

- Keywords that indicate high levels of emotion or that refer to serious problems that are unique to your product category;

- Complaints directed specifically at your company (denoted by messages that begin with your company's Twitter handle);

- Re-tweets of negative messages by people who are influential in your market.

Listening should be a companywide effort, not just a marketing task, and it should cover more than just Twitter and Facebook. B2B companies learned this early. A lot of them see little discussion of their brands or products in popular social networks, but they see plenty of action in professional communities. These forums may be accessible to only paid or qualified members, and the only way to tap into them is for a human being to visit them regularly.

Discussions also take place in media that aren't easily indexed by search engines, such as audio or video. You may learn of the discussion from Twitter, but to really understand it you have to watch the video on YouTube, where you'll also be privy to the pre-teen trash talk that seems to dominate conversations there. That isn't one of YouTube's more endearing features, but live with it.

The biggest potential time-waster is chasing down complaints about your brand that don't require response. We referred earlier to "Casual Complainers," who produce the bulk of negative sentiment for most companies. The people you assign to address online complaints need to have the experience and judgment to distinguish grumbling from cries of anguish. The fact is most people eventually figure out how to solve their own problems, so give them a chance. Don't let active listening create a support burden that wouldn't otherwise exist.

Train people in the response mechanisms we discussed in Chapter 4. When people complain, first thank them and then offer to try to set things right. If the conversation requires more than a quick acknowledgment, move it out of public view to e-mail or telephone. Show empathy, let people vent and don't lose your cool. Don't automatically take the blame, but promise to investigate the problem and get back to them with a timely response. Then do so. Always stress that you value their feedback, even if you're at an impasse. If the problem is systemic, then consider addressing it publicly via a blog post or e-mail. If it's *really* systemic, fix the product.

Dell Computer excels at listening. The company gets an average of 25,000 mentions of its brand in online channels every day (not counting "the farmer in the dell"), and it has developed a routing and response system to manage them. Dell uses Radian6 to track Twitter, Facebook, blogs, mainstream media and other major channels. Literally hundreds of employees have Radian6 accounts, and each has filters to detect conversations unique to their function.

Customer service listens for the brand name combined with keywords that indicate a serious problem, such as "won't start," "blue screen" or "about to throw this thing against the wall." Those customers may get a response proactively from a support rep. On the other hand, complaints about performance or software issues may not merit a response because the customer will eventually figure things out.

Product developers might listen for keywords such as "frustrating" or "overheat" because those indicate possible design shortcomings. Dell leaves decisions about whether and how to respond up to its people. Its policy manual spells out general guidelines for response, but the company ultimately trusts its employees' judgment.

Listening to social media is only one part of Dell's listening program. The company also maintains a virtual suggestion box called Ideastorm where anyone can submit a suggestion for vote by the community. Enterprise customers, who require a high degree of hands-on support, can go to Dell Tech Center and talk in real time to technologists who are trained in their complex and unique needs.[2]

What's the return on investment of all this? Richard Binhammer said the specific dollars and cents are less important than being tied into what customers are saying. "Social media positively impacts the customer lifecycle, and all that has an uplift to the business," he said. "It benefits Dell and the customer at each point in the lifecycle, from loyalty to return purchase to size of basket."

But it also helps to keep customers from catching on fire. Literally. Dell has caught and fixed numerous design problems — such as overheating in some of its Alienware laptops — after just a few weeks in the market because it was listening. This cuts down on expensive field replacements and recalls.

Active listening is like free market research. Customers are going to talk about you anyway, so why not tap into what they're saying? Responding to those conversations carries some risk, particularly in regulated industries, but listening is free. The trick is figuring out to whom you should listen.

The Customer Service Conundrum

In mid-2009, Paul's credit card was canceled because of an unspecified security breach. It was the third time in a year that the card had been voided, and Paul was miffed. He tweeted his annoyance with the big financial institution that held the account.

To his surprise, his tweet drew a nearly immediate response from a representative of the company. The rep asked Paul to follow him on Twitter and send a direct message describing his problem. Paul did as instructed and never heard from the rep or his company again.

About nine months later Paul was attending a dinner at the South by Southwest conference when the person across the table introduced himself as an employee of the credit card company. Paul told his story and was shocked to discover that his dinner companion was the same rep who had responded to his angry tweet months earlier. The man went on to explain that for months he had been the only authorized Twitter presence for his company, which is one of the world's largest financial institutions. The volume of messages was overwhelming, sometimes running to thousands in a day. Exhausted and overwhelmed, he eventually simply stopped responding to anyone.

Such an experience is all too common in the emerging world of social media customer service, where even the best companies still make up the rules as they go along. They also make lots of mistakes in the process. As businesses stumble and bumble their ways into these new channels, they're learning that customer expectations are quite different there than they were in the comfortable old world of call centers.

They have no choice but to learn. Social media is rapidly becoming a mainstream channel for solving customer problems. A 2012 survey of 2,000 U.K. consumers by Fishburn Hedges and Echo Research found 36% had interacted with companies through social media, nearly double the percentage of the year earlier. Of those who had interacted with companies in this way, 65% said they thought social media is a better way to communicate with companies than call centers, compared with just 7% who said the experience was worse.[3]

A 2012 study by Social Media Today, in cooperation with SAP and the Pivot Conference, found that seven out of eight businesses that use social media for customer service have seen a positive impact. Less than 1% described the experience as negative.[4]

The way companies are coping with these new channels differs widely, however. The phenomenon is so new that few best practices exist. Also, few businesses are organized to deliver customer service in a public forum.

For the first decade of the Web, most organizations treated the Internet as a channel to deliver a message and invested control in the department that does that best — marketing. The commercial Web is now maturing into a two-way channel, but the newswire mentality dies hard.

Research firm A.T. Kearney examined the top 50 branded Facebook pages in 2011 and found that 47 of them directed visitors to a one-way communication channel. That number was actually up from 46 in 2010. Kearney also found that 28 of the brands did not respond to a single visitor comment on Facebook during the entire year, a number that was unchanged from 2010. On average, more than six in 10 posts by companies on their own Facebook pages were overtly promotional in nature, despite the fact that such content generated only 11% of customer responses.[5]

ThinkJar and Sword Ciboodle surveyed 400 U.S. and U.K. companies with medium to large contact centers and found that 60% had adopted either Twitter or Facebook for customer service. Among those that had chosen either platform, 85% had adopted both. "However, adoption seems to have been the easy part," the researchers reported. "Justification, integration and strategic measurement continue to be the most challenging aspects of implementing new social channels."

Comcast's PR Coup

Frank Eliason is widely credited with kicking off the social-for-service trend. In 2008, he came up with the idea of using Twitter to respond to customer service problems about his employer, Comcast, where Eliason held the title of director of digital care. Comcast had good reason to try some new ideas; its reputation for customer service was so bad that at one point, the majority of results for a Google search on "Comcast customer service" were hate sites and customer rants. In 2004 and 2007, it had the worst customer satisfaction rating of any company or government agency in the country, including the Internal Revenue Service, according to the American Customer Satisfaction Index (ACSI).

Eliason began monitoring Twitter for keywords that indicated customer problems and responding proactively, often in minutes. It was the early days of Twitter, and many of the complaining customers were digerati who weren't shy about airing their gripes. One of them was TechCrunch founder Michael Arrington. Working under the Twitter handle @ComcastCares, Eliason intercepted an annoyed tweet from the prominent blogger and arranged to have his problems fixed in a jiffy. Arrington gushed about the experience, and Comcast enjoyed some much-needed positive PR.

Comcast continued to press its first-mover advantage and now has more than 40 customer service representatives using Twitter. However, whether the company has actually moved the needle on customer service is debatable. A search for Comcast on Yelp in different geographic areas turns up a generally dismal rating, averaging about 1½ out of five stars. The #ComcastSucks hash tag still shows up many times each day on Twitter and Comcast's 2012 ACSI scores haven't budged in the four years since the Twitter initiative was launched. In fairness, most cable companies have pretty poor reputations for service.

ComcastCares was a publicity coup, however, that generated worldwide media coverage and made Eliason a darling of the social media set. Hundreds of copycats jumped into the fray, many without the slightest idea of what they were doing. Customer care on Twitter and Facebook is a public process that carries considerable risk. Once you start, you can't go back. Think before you start tweeting and organize on the back end. "As millions more catch on to this great route into traditional customer service channels, the challenge for brands will be maintaining the same level of service," said Eva Keogan, head of innovation at Fishburn Hedges, in a BBC report.[6]

Factors to Consider

The people you encounter in social media forums behave different-ly than typical customers. For one thing, they're more likely to share their experiences, both good and bad. The good news is that social media mavens are willing to spend, on average, 21% more with companies that provide excellent service compared with 11% for people who have never used social media for that purpose, ac-cording to the 2012 American Express Global Customer Service Barometer.[7] They also share stories about positive experiences with an average of 42 people compared with nine for typical customers.

The bad news is that active social media participants are also much more likely to abandon a purchase because of poor customer ser-vice (83% vs. 49%), and they tell an average of 53 others about a bad experience compared with 17 for people who stick to tradi-tional channels. On Twitter they can tell thousands, so you'd better have a process and a thick skin.

Think first about whether you want to encourage customers to gripe to the world instead of picking up the phone as they've al-ways done. Unless competitive pressures are forcing your hand, you might be better off keeping quiet and letting customers contact you through traditional channels. We believe all organizations should be listening to online conversations, but not all of them should be responding. If you're a health care company or financial institution, for example, there may be little you can say without running afoul of regulations. One pharmaceutical firm in Canada, where regulations are even tighter than in the U.S., told us it had a list of more than 200 words it couldn't use on Twitter or Facebook and that all posts had to be approved by the legal department. In communities that expect nearly instantaneous response, delay can be worse than saying nothing at all.

Then you need a process for guiding the complaint to a successful resolution, given that few problems can be resolved in blocks of 140 characters. We recommend you take complaints offline to e-mail or the phone as quickly as possible, keeping in mind that this may take longer and cost more than simply letting customers call your 800 number. You may actually find yourself dealing with more complaints because some customers who wouldn't bother to make a call won't think twice about sending a tweet.

You also have to consider the different expectations for time-to-resolution. Twitter has created an assumption of nearly instantaneous response. People who may have been content to wait a day or two for an e-mail to be returned get agitated if their tweet goes unanswered for more than an hour. A 2012 Edison Research survey of nearly 700 people who have contacted customer support by social media found that 32% expect a response within 30 minutes and 42% expect a response within 60 minutes.[8] Companies may enter the Twittersphere with great expectations for improving customer satisfaction and end up doing the opposite.

Once you're in for a penny with social media customer service, you're in for a pound. You need to listen on nights and weekends, and the people who are listening need to be empowered to take action. "No response can be quick enough, and the ability to act rapidly requires the constant, proactive monitoring of social media — on weekends, too," wrote McKinsey Quarterly. The upside, the authors note, is that "by responding rapidly, transparently, and honestly, companies can positively influence consumer sentiment and behavior."[9]

That last point is debatable. The Knowledge@Wharton website noted that the ACSI index of consumer contentment has moved up just one point since it was started in 1994, to 75.8 from 74.8.[10]

Satisfaction isn't the whole story, though. The real payoff of social media customer support can be in customer retention. Churn is a growing problem for many industries because customers have more choice than ever, and brand loyalty has been falling for years. In *A Complaint Is a Gift*, Janelle Barlow and Claus Møller argue that the most at-risk customers aren't those who complain but those who leave and never say anything. It's no secret that the cost of finding new customers is much higher than the cost of keeping the ones you already have. Social media are lowering the barriers to people airing their grievances, which means you have a better chance to intercept and retain brand defectors if you're actively engaging than if you're just listening. When it comes to measuring ROI, look at customer retention as a major measurement point.

Rise of the Influencers

Jenny Barnett Rohrs put aside a career as a music therapist a few years back to care for her kids. But she didn't put aside her passion for the art of crafting. "I cannot spend a day without creating something: music, a craft, a spot in the garden, a mess!" she told The Creative Connection blog. In 2009, she started sharing crafting tips on her own blog that she gave the tongue-in-cheek title of Craft Test Dummies (www.CraftTestDummies.com).

Barnett Rohrs was urged on by husband Jeff, an e-mail marketing executive who knows a thing or two about digital promotion. He coached Jenny to sweat the basics of writing good headlines, tagging content, updating her site frequently and using other social platforms to share her work. Jenny promoted her brand by volunteering to write for CraftCritique.com, a popular review site. She discovered that she particularly enjoyed writing reviews of crafting products, and over time she directed Craft Test Dummies in that direction.

She also spread her social wings. As of this writing, more than 4,400 people have registered their affinity for her Facebook page. The nearly 100 videos she's posted on YouTube have collectively been seen more than 133,000 times. She has 6,800 followers on Twitter and 1,400 on Pinterest. More than 1,000 people visit her site every day. She's even met Martha Stewart — twice.

Craft Test Dummies is the number three result on Google for "crafting reviews." Needless to say, Barnett Rohrs has no shortage of products to choose from. Just about every crafting company in the world beats a path to her door in hopes of getting a coveted endorsement. She gets paid for on-camera appearances for infomercials and crafting television shows, as well as to design and write crafting tutorials for e-books and company websites. The real moneymaker, however, is her consulting business. She contracts with crafting companies to teach them how to promote their brands in social media. Who's better qualified to teach them than someone who precisely matches the profile of the people they're trying to reach?

Barnett Rohrs is what communications pros call an influencer.[11] Every industry has them, and some — like crafting, cooking and child-rearing — have thousands. They're the people who have expertise but for a long time had no platform. Now they're the rock stars of the new media world. They're people you should get to know.

Flypaper for Search

Lately influencer relations has been a red-hot term in media relations circles, as communicators have finally realized that people other than journalists and celebrities influence buying decisions. That's because between 80% and 90% of product research decisions today begin with a search engine. Blogs are crack cocaine for search engines. Influence patterns began changing several years ago, but only recently has the trend sparked a minor feeding frenzy.

Influencers have special importance in a customer attack. The crisis point in most attacks occurs when the conversation jumps from social to mainstream media. There are several ways that can happen, but a tweet or a blog post by an influencer is the most common.

Popular bloggers like Michael Arrington (TechCrunch), Steve Rubel (Micro Persuasion), Robert Scoble (Scobleizer), Om Malik (GigaOm) and Gina Trapani (formerly of LifeHacker) have huge followings that include many of the top media. In specialized markets, including heavy industry, information technology and science, where trade publications have all but disappeared, the influence of bloggers is arguably even bigger. Computer security expert Bruce Schneier estimates his newsletter and blog reach about 250,000 readers each month. It used to require a small army of media pros to serve an audience of that size. Schneier does it by himself.

Many companies start influencer relations programs for marketing purposes, but one of the greatest values of these initiatives is defensive. Good influencer relations are insurance policies against attack. People who are active in social channels are the first ones to pick up on the rumbling that points to a developing problem. If you have a good relationship with them, they'll give you a heads-up.

Influencers are also some of the first people customers and the media consult when trying to understand a problem. Having a relationship with them won't necessarily prevent bad things from happening, but it makes it more likely that you'll get the benefit of the doubt. At the very least, it creates another channel of communication for you to use. So in addition to issuing a statement to the press, you can send personal e-mails or tweets to people on your influencer list with requests that they pass a message along to their followers. Some people will find the attention flattering. You're telling them they're important. And who doesn't like that?

Oversimplifying Influence

If you Google the phrase "influencer," you'll find most definitions refer to bloggers and people who have large social media followings. Some of these people are acquiring prominence within their fields of expertise that rivals that of traditional media, and their ability to move markets shouldn't be underestimated.

In addition to their own subscriber and follower lists, many bloggers are now sought after by media as opinion leaders. As we noted in Chapter 8, journalists now overwhelmingly turn first to search engines to find experts. Google's mysterious search engine favors bloggers because of their topical focus and personal tone.

The emergence of free influence measurement services such as Klout, Kred and PeerIndex have fueled interest in influencer relations. These services attempt to quantify influence by measuring things such as Twitter activity and blog comments. Consumer brands can use these services to find out who has built an audience for their thoughts on clothing, food or home design.

For technical or specialized topics, however, these services aren't very useful. That's because all the popular influence rating engines suffer from one common shortcoming: They penalize people who aren't active in social media. For example, Federal Reserve Chairman Ben Bernanke and Internet wunderkind Marc Andreessen aren't even rated on Klout because they use channels such as *The Wall Street Journal*, which Klout doesn't measure.[12]

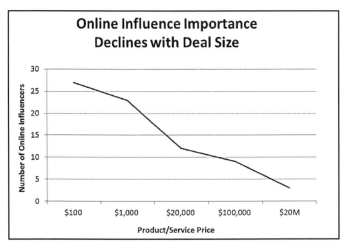

Source: Influencer50

People like to boil down complex issues to simple scores, and the temptation is to use Klout/Kred/PeerIndex and the lookalikes that will no doubt emerge as a baseline for deciding who deserves attention. We've even heard of companies screening job applicants based upon their Klout scores. We find this alarming because influence is situational, and not everyone chooses to play by the rules of these scoring engines.

Playing by the rules is one of the keys to success. The more social media practitioners tell the public measurement services about their activities, the better the chance they have of increasing their score.

Brian Solis of Altimeter Group quotes social media researcher danah boyd describing a fundamental weakness of this approach.

> *Klout, PeerIndex and similar services function through game mechanics. People who buy into the game are willing to manipulate their social media practices to get high status in these systems. But as they play the game — and as the companies respond to their gaming — those who are uninterested in the game end up getting written out of it. It evolves to be centered on the players.*[13]

Influence is a lot more complex than just social media activity, particularly in areas in which people don't share a lot of information publicly because of competitive or regulatory reasons. In their 2008 book, *Influencer Marketing: Who Really Influences Your Customers?*, Duncan Brown and Nick Hayes argue that some markets may be affected by as many as 50 different categories of influencers, ranging from regulators to academics to channel partners. The authors argue, in fact, that bloggers are relatively minor influencers relative to the knowledgeable authorities who have earned the trust of customers.

In a 2011 white paper, Brown and Hayes further dissected the influence equation by size of purchase. They found an inverse relationship between deal size and the number of online influencers. "As the price range moves into the five-figure bracket and beyond, then online influence plays a decreasingly small role, sometimes even non-existent," they wrote. "Why any significant marketing dollars are spent on trying to influence those in this buying cycle we really can't understand. It's totally unsupported using all the data available to us."[14] Business-to-business companies, in particular, should take these comments to heart.

The key point is that influence and audience are two different things. Celebrities can have huge audiences but little power to affect decisions. Conversely, people with very deep knowledge can have small audiences and great influence. Seth Godin said it well in the title of his 2006 book: *Small Is the New Big.*[15]

We believe social media influencers should be taken seriously and that their impact on markets can exceed the size of their following because they either have recognized domain expertise or strong personality appeal. However, you should resist the urge to boil this complex equation down to a number.

Whom and When to Engage

Influencer relations programs shouldn't kick in after a crisis begins. The process requires building trust and relationships. If you wait until your hair is on fire to approach prominent bloggers, you'll look like...well, like someone whose hair is on fire. And who wants to deal with a flaming person? Wait until the crisis has subsided and begin cultivating people in earnest.

The fact that people talk about your organization doesn't make them influential. Influence is a function of expertise, authority and credibility. Start by defining the audience you want to reach. Are they customers? Investors? Current or prospective partners? Government officials? Media? Each is probably influenced in different ways.

Put yourself in the shoes of the audience. Think about who shapes their opinions. These forces vary widely with the audience and market. For example, investment professionals are likely to pay much more attention to market analysts than to bloggers. Chief information officers trust the opinions of firms such as Gartner and Forrester Research, as well as their peers. On the other hand, young people buying sneakers may put their faith in the opinions of celebrity entertainers and their friends on Facebook. Each demands a different strategy. Some influencers are active in social or mainstream media and easy to identify. Others live in the shadows and are hard to find, like lichen. In high-ticket or highly regulated markets, they may not use social media at all. We maintain that if you're in the business of selling million-dollar MRI machines, your most effective social platform is the golf course.

When evaluating social media influence, here are some factors to consider:

Reach. This is a measure of total audience, and it's fairly easy to calculate when the influencer's activities are online-only. Here's where the Klouts of the world have value. The number of Twitter followers a person has is a good metric, but it's also one that is easily manipulated.[16] Look at the ratio of followers to people the influencer is following. The higher the ratio, the better. See how often the person is re-tweeted or mentioned by others.

Facebook "likes" are a poor metric of popularity because they can also be manipulated. Better measurements are shares and comments because they indicate engagement beyond simply clicking a button. Also look for a presence on YouTube, Google+, Pinterest, SlideShare and other social platforms that have a follower metaphor.

Blogs are more difficult to measure. Services such as Compete and Alexa estimate traffic and relative popularity, but their numbers are educated guesses at best. Some bloggers reveal metrics on their "About" pages or through advertising syndication services such as BlogAds and AdBrite, but you can also get a pretty good sense of influence by looking at the number of comments and shares on a writer's posts. Many bloggers display this data right on their entries. Assume that each comment is equivalent to about 100 readers.

Finally, an "about" page can also reveal influence factors. For example, many popular bloggers distribute their stuff through syndication services or regularly contribute to other blogs, which may have far greater reach than their own platforms. Third-party services such as paidContent.org, SeekingAlpha.com and Science-Blogs.com can greatly amplify a contributor's reach. Not all syndication services are the same, of course, and the worst ones don't even ask permission to republish. Look for services that screen prospective contributors or require a nomination process. The more stringent the rules, the better.

Search engine performance. Consider first whether search is important to the group you're trying to reach. It isn't always a factor. If you're a construction firm that specializes in building biotechnology labs, there's very little chance your customers are starting their decision process on Google (try the golf course). At the other extreme, few consumers consult search engines to figure out what brand of cola to buy. Nevertheless, search is crucial in many industries. If your product is the kind customers typically research before writing a check, then you need to be aware of who Google tells them is important.

Run queries on terms that your constituents are likely to use to get questions answered. The top results are probably people who frequently comment on your market and who have collected links from other credible sources. There's a pretty good chance they're influential. Pay close attention to choosing the right search terms. As search engine expert Mike Moran points out, people looking for a "hotel" are probably business travelers; people searching for "inn" are vacationers. Think like a customer.

Google favors frequently updated websites that show thematic consistency. The top results in a search engine query are likely to have a lot of links from other sites that cover the same topic. These are essentially "votes" for the content of the site, and they show that the author is credible. Use the Google "link" command to find out who is paying attention to the influencer. Entering "link:dietgirl.org" will show you links to that popular dieting blog. If you recognize the names, then the author is being read by people who matter.

Focus. Look at the stream of content that influencers publish. Does it indicate expertise and opinions about your market? Are their opinions likely to influence others to make decisions that matter to you? The fact that people talk a lot doesn't necessarily make them influential. In fact, the opposite is often true. You might also find that people aren't influential in areas you'd expect them to be. For example, there are a number of very active cooking bloggers who happen to have Ph.D.s in chemistry. Their bios might indicate that they're important people for pharmaceutical companies to know, but they write about flambés, not fluorocarbons. Kraft Foods might want to cozy up, but probably not Fischer Scientific.

Media attention. People who are influential in social media channels quickly attract the attention of the press. Many bloggers publish lists of press citations, and a search of their names will quickly show if they're frequently quoted in mainstream media (for example, "bruce schneier site:nytimes.com" yields some eye-popping results). Search video for archives of TV or video podcast appearances.

Popular bloggers are also likely to turn up on the speaking circuit. Their own websites may list past speaking engagements, and a search for the person's biography will turn up bios from conference programs.

Also check their publishing activity in more traditional channels. One of the first places publishers look for new authors these days is in the blogosphere because successful bloggers demonstrate domain expertise, ability to write and skill at building an audience. Authors are also likely to have television, radio and mainstream media coverage.

Biographies. Successful bloggers are only too happy to tell you about their success. Look at their "About" pages for details. Holly Becker started blogging in 2006 and today gets 48,000 visitors to decor8blog.com. She wrote a bestselling interior decorating book and was quoted in more than 15 major magazines in 2011 alone. How do we know that? It's all in the bio on her blog. Influential bloggers are also frequently interviewed by others. Googling their name may turn up insights you won't find anywhere else.

Managing an Influencer Relations Program

Integrating influencers into your existing communications programs doesn't have to be expensive or time-consuming. If the influencers are active in social media channels, make sure they are on your press list and are invited to the same events as the media. If they are people who exercise influence less publicly, such as resellers or regulators, have dedicated channels that address their specific needs, such as a newsletter or quarterly phone briefing.

Some companies take influencers so seriously that they commit significant resources to cultivating them. Software giant SAP has a section of its website dedicated to information and resources for social media and analyst influencers. It has even hosted events for those people.

Marketing automation vendor Eloqua unlocked a trove of once-proprietary intellectual property and gave it away for free to a group of hand-picked influencers. The people they selected were told they were members of an elite group chosen for their market influence, and their enthusiasm at spreading the word led to an immediate 43% increase in traffic to the Eloqua.com blog and a 21% increase in online demonstrations, which are the company's most important leading purchase indicator.[17]

Unlike media, many influencers are flattered to be asked to assist your company. Consider creating an advisory board to periodically give you feedback and help you with problem situations. Consult the board routinely — at least twice a year. Don't assemble the group only when under attack. Offer non-cash rewards if you can, such as early information about new products or promotion for their businesses. If you feel compensation is needed, keep it modest. A few shares of stock or branded items from your company store usually suffice.

A Few Pointers

Get your own house in order first. Before you even begin an influencer program, make sure you use the channels they use. Many social media enthusiasts prefer Twitter and Facebook to e-mail and telephone. They'd rather follow you or subscribe to your RSS feed than wait for you to contact them. Be sure you communicate through all relevant channels, and make it easy for them to subscribe to your content if that's their preference.

Make it personal. In Chapter 3, we told the story of how Ford Motor Company's Scott Monty defused a crisis within hours by working his network of personal contacts. Not every company is lucky enough to have a Scott Monty, but you should make influencer relations a person-to-person affair.

Incidentally, mail merge is not personal. Sending out canned messages complimenting bloggers on the "excellent insight you showed in [post name here]" is only going to piss people off. You can't fake this stuff. It's better to make your influencer list smaller than to try to automate relationships. Once you get a reputation as a spammer, it's almost impossible to recover.

Treat influencers the same way you would the media. Some companies worry that this is a slippery slope: If they legitimize *any* bloggers by treating them like media, then they have to treat all bloggers the same. Nonsense. Decide what criteria a person needs to meet in order to merit special treatment, and be prepared to explain those criteria to people who might object. As long as your criteria make sense, you're covered.

At the same time, remember that influencers *aren't* traditional media. Media pros know the rules and the wink-wink-nudge-nudge games of public relations. Influencers don't. You need to understand what they care about and show that you care, too.

In a case of a blogger, scanning a few recent posts, reading a biography and noting the categories or tags the person uses can give you a quick idea of what motivates him or her. For someone who contributes to a group blog, consult his or her profile and list of recent posts to learn this information.

Make your initial contact meaningful and positive. If the e-mail address isn't on the site, use a search engine, Zoominfo.com, Spock.com or LinkedIn to find it. Or just post a comment. Even if you don't like what the writer says about your organization, find something you do like and say something nice. After all, you're trying to make friends with these folks.

Offer something of value. The best way to interest influencers is with information that has value. Give them stuff to post on their blogs, Pinterest accounts or YouTube channels. You don't need a full-blown social media newsroom to do this, but you do need to be aware that online influencers work in multiple media. This is particularly true in consumer markets. Develop your content with an eye toward graphics, slideshows, audio and video that they can plug and play into whatever media they use.

And go easy on the giveaways. There's nothing wrong with hosting an open bar at a trade show event, but avoid extravagant gifts.

They may backfire on you. The Federal Trade Commission adopted standards in 2010 that require bloggers to disclose compensation received as an incentive for coverage. Even before those rules went into effect, many had already adopted informal policies that were at least as restrictive.

Follow through. Designate a person or people to own relationships, and make it a point to connect with key influencers at least quarterly. This can be as simple as re-tweeting a message or posting a comment on a well-crafted blog entry. Seriously, an hour a year is all you need to maintain the relationship.

Expect to be challenged. Unlike reporters, who are usually dispassionate about the companies they cover, bloggers are enthusiastic, knowledgeable and fueled by feedback from their committed readers. They ask smart questions, and they see themselves as champions of a new media form that deserves attention. Asked by Technorati why they blog, 70% said it was "to share my expertise and experience with others." That's a pretty powerful motivation.

Once you tap into the online channels that matter in your market and engage with the right people, you're in a strong position to fend off an online attack. Let's go there next.

Chapter 10: Handling an Attack

We hope that if you've stuck with us this far, you've picked up on a few threads that run throughout this book:

- Bad things happen to good companies. Johnson & Johnson, Procter & Gamble, Ford, the meat processing industry and many others were all doing legal, ethical things when they came under attack. The fact that your heart is in the right place doesn't mean someone won't try to rip it from your body.

- There's no time to think in a crisis anymore. It used to be you had the benefit of at least a day or two to craft a response. Now you get grief if you don't talk within an hour. You must be prepared for the most likely attack scenarios because the Internet no longer affords you time to craft a thoughtful strategy. Your response must be almost reflexive.

- Silence isn't an option. The more quickly and openly you deal with a crisis, the faster it goes away.

- Transparency is essential. Don't lie and don't assume. Ever. If you don't know the facts, say so.

- When responding to a crisis, you used to speak to media professionals with whom you had established relationships or who at least understood the rules of engagement. Now you don't even know who the media are. Bloggers may have influence that exceeds all but the largest newspapers. There are no rules of engagement. In some cases, the media you respond to are also the people attacking you.

- Attacks can come out of nowhere and quickly grow out of proportion. The beef industry had used lean finely textured beef for a decade before the ingredient suddenly became a business nightmare. A Chick-fil-A executive's comments on anti-gay rights touched off a debate over tolerance that impacted the 2012 presidential campaign.

- Nearly anyone can start an attack, and people try to do so every day. It's almost impossible to predict when the problem will escalate from one irate customer to a national media storm.

- Your goodhearted attempts to resolve an issue can create bigger problems. Private communications between you and an angry customer get posted on Reddit for others to mock. You try to resolve problems on Twitter and create an unsustainable customer service precedent. You fire the employee who screwed up and start a conspiracy theory.

- Facebook is the devil. Not really. Just kidding.

In this chapter, we tell you how to put plans, policies and procedures in place to handle an attack that originates in social media. Few companies plan for reputational crises at all. They'd rather devote their departmental off-site meetings to happy topics such as growth and leadership. That's fine, but taking a half-day once every couple of years to talk about and rehearse attack responses seems like a good time investment to us.

Altimeter Group estimates that more than three-fourths of social media attacks can be diminished or averted if organizations simply prepare for the most-likely scenarios. A lot of this is just common sense and taps into the knowledge that employees bring to work with them every day. It doesn't have to take long, and once the program is in place, it can be revisited and revised as part of an occasional operational review.

Prepare for the Predictable

Most attack scenarios are pretty easy to predict. Think of your business. What problems could negatively impact sales or customer perceptions? What crises have your competitors or predecessors endured? Abstract these situations to a higher level, and you'll probably find there are just a handful of factors that are common to them.

Some are industry-specific. The food industry frets about contamination. Airlines worry about planes crashing. Financial services firms want to avoid looking greedy. Utilities prepare for power outages. All of those crises have existed for years. The difference now is that more people talk about them, and it's easier for misinformation to flourish.

Here are some essentials for preparing scenarios:

Know your product. If what you do could ever be perceived to present public health hazards, then you need a plan of action in case someone decides to make trouble. The attack could begin as a research study, a famous person with an ax to grind or even just a lowly blogger. Think of the worst-case scenario: What would you do if a scientific study found your product causes cancer? How would you respond in the first hour, the first day and during the first week? If you're prepared for that worst case, then the more likely scenarios are easier to manage.

Know your people. If your business involves frequent contact with customers you don't know very well, consider the worst damage a single employee encounter could cause. This should guide your customer service training, but it should also challenge you to come up with response and disciplinary scenarios, remembering that firing people isn't always the answer. Enlist an employee or consultant to play the role of an angry customer and rehearse the most-likely attack scenes, using the response tactics outlined in Chapter 4.

Know your partners. Consider the suppliers and distributors with whom you do business and whether they're a potential liability. Are there any skeletons in their closet that could embarrass you? Can they be counted on to support you in a crisis, or at least stay quiet? Is the CEO a loose cannon? Have they fully disclosed to you their customer list and their financial relationships? Remember that the media will point fingers at you for failing to exercise judgment over the companies you do business with, particularly if you're a large company.

Know your industry. Your competitor's embarrassment may be a scene-setter for your own. The news media love to look for linkages between events, even if the connections are fragile. The Exxon Valdez and Deepwater Horizon oil spills were nightmare scenarios for the energy industry. Any company's response to a future crisis of that kind will be compared to Exxon and BP. Don't repeat others' mistakes. Also, know what people expect of companies like yours. People have lower expectations of airlines than they do of jewelers. The crisis scenarios are also different, as are the expectations people put on you.

Know popular sentiment. Alarm over America's obesity crisis has made the past few years a tricky time to launch a high-calorie food product. A small change in popular culture can quickly turn negative even on successful products. For example, the 2004 film "Super Size Me" has been credited with forcing McDonald's to eliminate the term "Super Size" from its vocabulary and starting a menu review that rippled through the entire fast food industry.

Sometimes you can prosper by going against the grain. Burger King's bacon sundae, which weighed in at 510 calories and 18 grams of fat, was hardly a politically correct product to introduce at the height of concerns about American obesity in 2012, but it got lots of attention for Burger King. General Motors was pilloried by environmentalists for the Chevy Tahoe campaign described in Chapter 5, but GM didn't really care. The critics would never have bought the vehicle in the first place, and the negative publicity actually generated lots of awareness with the audience GM was trying to reach.

The point isn't to do what's politically correct but to understand what people think about your business or industry and how that will affect the way they perceive your actions.

Get Your Social Assets in Order

Social media has made attack planning vastly more complex. It has created dozens of new attack vectors and made active listening a communications imperative. The good news is you can use the same channels as your attackers to craft a response. The bad news is few companies even know what channels they have.

We know of one big technology company that has more than 400 branded Twitter accounts and more than 130 Facebook pages and groups. The company's decentralized management strategy gives its brands and geographies wide latitude to manage their own online presences. The problem is there is no federation between them. There's no requirement for account-holders to register their branded presence with a central authority, and the company doesn't even have a comprehensive list of who's responsible for which accounts.

This situation is not uncommon. The mad rush to get into social media over the past few years has caused many organizations to put action ahead of governance. We applaud their willingness to experiment, and we think a decentralized strategy is the only way to go. Social media is all about connecting people in small communities. Layers of overhead introduce delay and confusion. Also remember that you don't have the luxury of time anymore.

"It is important [that] it doesn't take three days and 1,654 e-mails to decide how to respond to, for example, one lousy comment it took some heartless bastard 30 seconds to post," wrote Lisa Gerber, chief content officer at the Spin Sucks Pro blog, in a post on Social Media Sun.[1]

However, social channels now have an impact that demands some discipline. We think it's possible to have the best of both worlds if you put good policies and training in place and know who's speaking for you.

The social network providers aren't going to help you control your brand. Facebook doesn't verify that someone who wants to set up a branded page has authority to do so. It's the same with Twitter and Google+. You may be able to wrest a page away from an impostor, but the process can take months. You should plant a brand flag in every social network of any importance to you before somebody else does. Even if you don't actively update the account, at least you own it.

If you're a large company, you probably have a lot more branded presences than you know, particularly if you have international subsidiaries. Designate someone to create a master list of those accounts. Make sure the people who administer them know where to go to find out how to respond to a crisis. Your social media policy should stipulate that no one is authorized to speak on behalf of the company without written permission to do so.

Here are some of the major platforms where your brand may be represented. Do you know the status of all of them?

- Facebook accounts

- Facebook pages

- Branded Twitter accounts

- Independent Twitter accounts of people who represent themselves as your employees

- LinkedIn company profiles

- LinkedIn groups

- Pinterest accounts[2]

- YouTube accounts

- Flickr accounts

- SlideShare accounts and pages

- Instagram accounts

- Managers of communities you own

- Authorized representatives in communities you don't own

- Forum administrators

- Authorized company bloggers

- Independent bloggers who represent themselves as your employees

Those are just the big fish. There are lots of smaller or topical social networks that also support branded presences. While your interns are busy working Google to put that list together, here are some other tasks to attend to.

Create a social media policy. You mean you don't have one yet? You should, and a policy isn't that hard to create. Many companies publish their social media policies, and you can easily adapt best practices from some of the world's biggest brands. Chris Boudreaux' Social Media Governance (socialmediagovernance.com) has a large collection of policies, as well as guidelines for creating your own. The Word Of Mouth Marketing Association's Guide to Disclosure in Social Media Marketing is a must-read guide to best practices in social media policies.[3]

The best policies give employees a lot of freedom to promote the company and help solve customer problems, but they also put limitations in place. Employees should always disclose their affiliation and should never represent themselves as a company spokesman unless authorized. They should keep their comments positive and never mention competitors and specific customers. Experienced bloggers and community administrators are usually granted some flexibility, but they should be the exception.

The fact that people operate under pseudonyms or don't disclose their company affiliation in some places doesn't exempt them from your policy. If they can be traced back to you, they're your problem. The moment anyone reveals that they work for you in any online context, they should operate under your policy. Google makes it very difficult to hide your identity these days.

Special guidelines apply to employees who administer branded accounts. Authoring tools that automate the posting of information across multiple accounts can be a booby trap. In early 2011, Chrysler fired its social media agency over a single tweet sent by an employee that insulted Detroit drivers. The timing was bad because Chrysler had just debuted a new ad campaign celebrating Detroit.

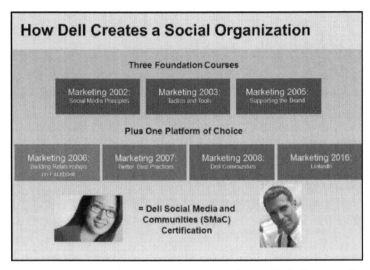

Source: Dell Computer, Inc.

The employee intended to send the tweet using his personal Twitter account, but he checked the wrong box on his smart phone and used the branded @ChryslerAutos account by mistake. Tools such as HootSuite and Spredfast make putting your foot in your mouth one-button simple.

Dell Computer, PepsiCo and Sprint are among the growing number of companies that are formalizing social media training as part of their HR education programs.[4] Dell's Social Media and Communities (SMaC) Certification requires participants to complete three foundation courses and one platform-specific specialty course.

Know who's speaking for you. When employees sign the social media policy, they should disclose all social network accounts they maintain. You should create a master listening list of all these accounts in a tool such as HootSuite or Radian6 and keep an eye on it. You aren't violating anybody's privacy by doing this because the conversations are public. You're just keeping tabs on what your people are saying.[5]

This step is also important because it tells you where your communication points are in case you need to get to them. A crisis situation demands that everyone be on the same page, and that includes individual employees with their blogs and Twitter accounts. They should either deliver a consistent message or clam up, depending on what the situation demands. All it takes is one person playing Lone Ranger to say the wrong thing and escalate a problem.

Federate your social presences. Some of the most embarrassing attacks of recent years happened because individuals who were authorized to represent the company publicly took matters into their own hands. When attackers mass on your Facebook page, it shouldn't be up to the administrator to decide what to do. Anyone who manages a branded social account should be trained in how to deal with a crisis situation. A good rule: When in doubt, notify corporate communications.

Any branded account should have two or more administrators. At least one of those administrators should be a corporate communications professional or an account owned by the communications department. Imagine the nightmare of a disgruntled employee using a corporate Facebook account to attack his employer. This happened to one of Paul's clients. The company owned a network of retail stores, each of which had its own locally maintained Facebook page. The company fired one of its store managers in an acrimonious dispute and only then discovered that he had sole control of the store's Facebook page, which he was using to trash his former employer. It took months to get back control of the page from the notoriously unresponsive Facebook. The lesson: Never give anyone sole control of your brand. Anywhere.

Set up a coordination point to communicate instructions and updates in the event of a problem. *Don't use e-mail for this purpose.* Distribution lists quickly go out of date, and e-mail is easily misfired or intercepted by the wrong people. A private LinkedIn group is sufficient for most situations. It's a quick and easy way to communicate to a large number of people, and you can control the membership. If you set up such a group, stop using e-mail for this purpose. You need to force people to use the group so they don't fall back to old habits.

159

Documents can be shared with free and low-cost services such as Google Docs or Microsoft SkyDrive. If security is a critical issue, paid document-sharing services such as Firmex and ShareFile provide secure access control and auditing.

Define roles and responsibilities. A well-crafted crisis plan defines clearly what individuals should do, including those designated to speak as well as those who *shouldn't* speak.

When an attack occurs, the response should be managed by as few people as possible while leveraging as many outlets as are appropriate. Respond to critics only in the places they attack. There's no reason to create a perception of trouble where one doesn't exist. Your communications people should use their social profiles to respond, as well as the organization's profiles. Personal contacts matter, and the social capital that people build by being good online citizens can be invaluable when a crisis strikes. Think of Scott Monty and The Ranger Station.

RightNow Technologies had a "communication committee" that met monthly, but it could be called together 24/7 in case of emergency. The committee consisted of senior management, PR and investor relations personnel, customer service and marketing leaders. Basically, anyone who might be required to respond to a crisis was represented. There was a three-level coding system — red, orange, and yellow — for three levels of crisis. Each defined the characteristics of a crisis at that level and the required speed with which they had to respond. For example, red and orange meetings could be called by anyone, and the meeting had to take place within two hours.

If you have an influencer relations program in place, be sure that individuals in your organization are assigned to groups of influencers. They may need to leverage those personal relationships to help put out a fire.

Prepare scenarios. A half-day of brainstorming can produce the most likely attack scenarios. Group them into three categories:

- **Category Three** risks are those that can significantly damage the company's operations or reputation. For example, if customers are injured by defects in a product (as happened with Toyota's 2010 brake problems) or if an executive is caught trying to manipulate the company's stock price (as the CEO of Whole Foods did), the company may lose sales, face litigation or suffer long-term damage to its valuation. These scenarios need to be handled by a small number of communication professionals, usually in cooperation with legal staff and top executives. Social channels need to be carefully controlled.

- **Category Two** risks cause disruption or embarrassment and may temporarily depress sales or stock price, but they aren't lethal threats to the business. These problems can usually be handled without legal staff, but corporate management may have to get involved. You'll need to identify spokespeople who can be quickly enlisted to speak on behalf of the company. They should be believable, articulate and photogenic. They should also have a sense of humor.

- **Category One** risks are annoying but not damaging. These problems may generate publicity, but they probably aren't going to stop people from doing business with you. Frontline staff can usually handle them with the proper procedures in place. Category One risks can graduate to Category Two if your response isn't appropriate, however. You need to train people who deal with customers directly in the basics of customer relations, keeping in mind that 40% of attacks originate at this level.

Practice attack response. The Weber Shandwick public relations firm has a novel service for its customers called Firebell. It creates a simulated crisis in which clients must react in real time to information cascading in on them from hate blogs, rogue videos, Twitter messages, reporters on deadline and even flash mobs. Some 30 to 40 people may be involved in the drill, which simulates a four-day event in about four hours. Participants use a dashboard that enables them to receive and post simulated messages to social channels. In the meantime, Weber Shandwick professionals constantly conjure up new plot twists to throw at them.

"We intentionally put clients in a situation where they have to research answers," said David Krejci, executive vice president of social media and digital communications at Weber Shandwick. "One company faced a claim that they were testing on animals when they weren't. The point is to respond quickly while also investigating the facts."

Krejci said some clients emerge shaken from the exercise, and many don't even remember everything that happened. The simulation dramatizes to large companies in particular the importance of coordinating between headquarters and local operations. "If a flash mob happens a thousand miles away, people have to coordinate what's going on at the store with what they're thinking at corporate," Krejci said. "It may sound like a good idea at headquarters to get the cops out to disperse the crowd, but it could be a nightmare for people trying to manage things on-site."

You don't need an exercise as sophisticated as Firebell to rehearse a crisis response. You can get pretty close using whiteboards and slips of paper. Your team needs to get a feeling for what it's like when information is cascading in from all sides and no one knows what's what. Everyone needs to know exactly what his or her role is, where to go for information and which channels to use. This is a great team-building exercise to try during your next departmental retreat.

The Four Stages of Crisis

Now that you've done your homework, here's how to put the tools to use. Customer attacks usually follow a predictable trajectory. Catalysts may be a confrontation with a customer, bad behavior by an executive or employee, a research report that casts a product in an unfavorable light or an act of protest by an organization. As we noted in Chapter 4, negative customer experiences are the most common cause.

What follows the triggering event is usually a frenzied period of fact-finding and contextualizing, as the target of the attack tries to get the facts straight while critics, analysts and interested bystanders

Checklist for Attack

Paul Fox, director of corporate communications at Procter & Gamble, offers these eight tips for dealing with a crisis:

- Focus on your real audiences and ensure you have the right channels to communicate with them.

- Own up to mistakes and don't try to own the message.

- Always tell the truth. Everything you say will be shared.

- Be prepared to revisit your business and demonstrate your willingness to change.

- Optimize on negative keywords.

- Set up a (dark) crisis response blog.

- Make press releases supplementary to social media responses.

- It's never too early to engage in social media in preparation for future crises.

speculate about what it all means. Once the facts are in focus, the action moves to blame and consequences. The final stage — aftermath — can last a painfully long time.

In her book, *The Four Stages of Highly Effective Crisis Management*, Jane Jordan-Meier outlines a four-stage process by which crises typically unfold. We will use this as a roadmap for response and for deploying your social media channels appropriately.

Searching for Facts

Stage One is the Fact-Finding Stage. These days, social media is often the first outlet to report on an incident, and mainstream media engage in a feeding frenzy trying to get the facts while also competing to be first to report new developments.

This is a hectic time because you probably don't know any better than anyone else what's going on. Don't assume the story that's being told in social channels is correct, but do take it seriously. You can issue an official corporate statement, but you should also use the channels your attackers are using. Stick to those channels, and don't bring new platforms into the mix. There's no reason to create awareness where it doesn't already exist.

Send out tweets, blog entries and/or Facebook posts that make it clear you're looking into the matter. One of the advantages of using social channels is that they're informal and fast. Issuing a press release at Stage One may call undue attention to an issue that turns out to be nothing. Use your social channels to put down a marker. Then follow up.

If possible, make the author of the statements a person or people rather than a brand. Here's where a trusted presence can help. In the same way that professional communicators use their media relationships to manage a story, your people should leverage their credibility in social channels to ask for time to correct misinformation. Wait to issue a formal statement until you're sure you need to.

Don't wait to gather all the facts before making a statement. No one expects that in the early hours of a crisis anyway. It's more important to show that you're trying to get to the bottom of the issue and that you'll update people as you go along. Then do that.

"Resist the temptation to speculate," Jordan-Meier wisely advises.[6] Credibility is critical at this stage. Don't assume the people you thought were above reproach aren't capable of doing the wrong thing. A lot of people thought Penn State football icon Joe Paterno was too good to cover up for a pedophile on his staff. Look how fast that image of perfection crumbled.

Your advantage in Stage One is that no one expects you to have the answers. They do expect you to say something, though. Keep these guidelines in mind:

Resolve in private, if possible. If the problem affects just a few people, ask them to contact you in private. You can do this on Twitter by asking people to follow you and then send a direct message with an e-mail address or phone number to resolve the issue out of public view.

Show empathy. You can demonstrate concern without admitting guilt. Express regret for any harm or inconvenience that has occurred.

Make the message personal. Use bylines and video statements with real people whenever possible. Don't do what Progressive Insurance did in the case described in Chapter 3. Amid an emotionally supercharged atmosphere, the company issued a robotic statement under a corporate byline.[7] We can't imagine a worse way to deal with a human tragedy.

Limit the number of social accounts you use to communicate, and be consistent. Don't make people hunt around for information. It's fine to re-tweet via other accounts that you own.

Address affected parties, not spectators. The peanut gallery on Twitter can be relentless, but they're not your constituency. Speak about what you're doing to help people with issues. The one exception to this is people who have large followings. If they're agitating against you, but aren't directly affected by the crisis, engage with them directly and ask for their help in communicating the facts.

Consider creating a website or blog post to report progress. This is particularly useful if the problem is systemic, such as an outage or recall. Instead of trying to respond personally to every inquiry, send a link to a page with the latest information. Consider creating a unique Twitter hash tag that people can follow for updates.

Also keep in mind that whatever you say will be run through the wringer of public investigation and debate. Don't make a statement like "BPA is used in the lining or lid of most metal food cans in the U.S." unless you're absolutely sure it's true.[8] Also, be cautious about language that could be interpreted as lecturing, scolding or condescending. Remain humble throughout the course of an attack.

Don't try to contain embarrassing or inflammatory information about a crisis at Stage One. Once the truth comes out — as it inevitably will — you'll have the additional problem of defending your cover-up.

There were 6 billion mobile phone subscriptions in the world at the end of 2011, and most of those devices have cameras. Thinking you can keep information under wraps where nearly everyone is a potential video producer is folly. Officials at Virginia Tech initially withheld information about a gunman's 2007 rampage in hopes that they could resolve the situation internally, but they couldn't stop witnesses from transmitting video of the violence to CNN. Penn State officials hoped to deal with allegations of child rape by one of its football coaches internally. The cover-up eventually took down the university's president and several other top administrators.

Professional communicator, blogger and podcaster Neville Hobson said it best in a speech to the Public Relations Institute of Ireland in April 2012: If you fail to disclose relationships that are important to the story, then you will be found out.[9] Once you are, your failure to disclose will become a bigger story than the one you want to tell.

Hobson is emphatic about the futility of trying to control social media, saying such efforts "inevitably lead to disaster." Some prominent efforts to do this have become the butt of jokes and worse. In 2012, the French government made it illegal for people to speculate about the open results of the presidential election before the polls closed. Twitter users thumbed their nose at the rule, concocting code words about football and cooking that clearly referred to the candidates.[10] Similarly, when a British soccer player obtained a "superinjunction" against media disclosure of his name or details of an extramarital affair, the rule was openly flouted on social media channels that aren't subject to British law.

It's hard to keep cool at the early crisis stage, particularly if social media is beginning to combust. No matter: Stick to what you know and dispel misinformation. Think back to other incidents that may be similar to yours. What can you learn from them and how might that affect your response strategy?

Looking for Answers

Jordan-Meier labels Stage Two "the Unfolding Drama," but it might just as well be called "Feeding Frenzy." This is when the basic facts have been verified and people are looking to assess blame. If there are victims — whether indignant customers or people who have been physically injured — the media will focus on them. Expect to hear tales of human emotion with your organization as villain.

Speculation and rumor still run rampant at this stage. Use the same channels and tactics outlined in Stage One. Talk often about what you're doing to resolve the crisis and any wins you achieve. Make it clear that your number one concern is for victims, not your organization. Of all the sound bites that came out of the 2010 Gulf oil spill, none will be better remembered than CEO Tony Hayward's "I'd like my life back." Those five words betrayed an arrogance that undermined everything BP did from that point on to manage the crisis. It was clear to everyone that Hayward's job would not survive the spill.

This is where your influencer relations program pays off. Know which experts are on your side, and contact them so they'll be up to date if the media call. Under no circumstances should you try to "coach" experts or dangle the possibility of a reward. Anything that could be perceived as sneaky or manipulative will simply become part of the bigger case against you.

This is also a good time to start the "just the facts" website mentioned earlier. Use the same headlines, tags and keywords that your critics use so that your defense will turn up in the same search results as your critics' attack. That's what DuPont did in 2007 to deal with persistent reports that its Teflon nonstick coating caused cancer. TeflonIsSafe.com used an FAQ format and neutral language to relate the results of many studies about Teflon's safety while emphasizing "Consumers can use their cookware with complete confidence." The rumor still crops up years later, but DuPont's "just the facts" approach effectively contained the crisis in the early going.

You should also have your most credible and sympathetic spokespeople at the ready. YouTube can be your friend in a crisis, particularly if the broadcast media aren't cooperating. You want people who can look earnestly into the camera and deliver a heartfelt explanation or apology. They should be people who are in a position to make changes, if necessary. Don't over-script these statements. Videos should communicate empathy and concern. It's okay if the wording isn't perfect.

Blame Game

Jordan-Meier says Stage Three — the "Finger-Pointing Stage" — is the one you want to avoid at all costs. There is no upside for you in playing a blame game, and silence is your greatest enemy.

Stage Three occurs when a crisis is in full flower and everyone has an opinion, mostly negative. The media look for scapegoats and pit parties against each other. The history of your organization is examined for evidence of systemic weakness or executive incompetence that enabled the crisis to develop. Your lack of response is seen as an admission of guilt.

The crisis at the Komen for the Cure that we described in Chapter 2 is an example of how *not* to manage this stage. Komen's silence left a vacuum that was filled with other people's speculation. It was perceived as an admission of guilt and became such a focus of attention that when officials finally did speak, few people believed them.

When bad behavior is at the root of a problem, many executives default to a knee-jerk response: Fire the bastard. Disciplinary action may make things worse, though.

America Online probably thought it was being decisive when it terminated the irritating customer service rep who refused to cancel Vincent Ferrari's account in the famous attack described in Chapter 6. It failed to get the message that the villain in the story wasn't the rep but the company itself.

The company would have done better to take the route FedEx did when an employee was caught on a security camera tossing a computer monitor over a customer's fence in late 2011. Instead of firing the driver, the company put forth a well-dressed and articulate executive to frame the incident as a completely unacceptable breakdown in procedure and to restate the company's commitment to customer respect.[11] While FedEx disciplined the driver, it didn't fire him. It chose to put the greater blame on itself for failing to enforce its procedures more rigorously. FedEx's response looked deliberate and mature, while AOL's looked panicked.

The best way to avoid getting to Stage Three is to manage Stage Two well. Speak early and often, and make it clear you're on top of the issue. "If you [wait to] stick your head out in [Stage Three] — typically 72 hours after the incident first happened — God help you; you will be crucified by the media," wrote Jordan-Meier. "You need to speak early and often."

Aftermath

Stage Four comes when the bleeding has stopped and attention turns to lessons learned and next steps. This is a time of reflection, when you need to consider whether structural changes need to be made to prevent a recurrence. It is not a time to relax. The worst thing to do at the end of a crisis is go back to life as usual. The media and the public may demand accountability, and people may have to be fired. You need to communicate what actions will be taken to strengthen the company against another attack. The nightmare scenario is if the same crisis happens again.

Is Astroturfing Ever Appropriate?

Astroturfing is a fake grassroots movement intended to "give the impression of spontaneous support for an idea/product/company/service," according to the Chartered Institute of Public Relations (CIPR).[12] It may involve paying influencers to express a particular point of view, spreading rumors or creating organizations or websites that appear genuine but have a secret agenda.

Although many astroturfing campaigns have been exposed and embarrassed the companies that created them, the practice continues. As recently as May 2011 Burson Marsteller was exposed for pitching bloggers to write articles critical of Google's privacy policies.

Chick-fil-A was accused of "sock puppetry," a form of astroturfing, in the controversy around its support of anti-gay organizations in 2012. As critics massed on Facebook, a teenager named Abby Farle came to the restaurant's defense. But Abby Farle didn't exist. Her account had been created only a day earlier, and critics quickly tracked her profile picture to a stock photo website. Chick-fil-A vigorously denied that Abby was its creation. We may never know the truth. It's even possible that Abby was created by a Chick-fil-A attacker to make the company look guilty of sock puppetry.

A glance at Wikipedia's extensive list of Astroturfing examples should be evidence enough that this practice is a bad idea,[13] particularly for commercial companies. Political organizations practice a more subtle form of Astroturfing because campaign-finance laws regulate direct contributions to candidates. The practice is more accepted in politics because, basically, everybody does it.

Chapter 11: The Attack-Resistant Organization

Shortly after the first Gulf War in 1991, insurance company USAA sent refund checks to thousands of customers without being asked. The company, which principally served military personnel at the time, reasoned that troops stationed overseas weren't in a position to drive their cars and so shouldn't be charged insurance premiums while they were abroad. Customers were so delighted at the gesture that some 2,500 of them sent the checks back, saying that the knowledge that the company would always be there for them was sufficient reward. Not surprisingly, USAA has long enjoyed some of the highest customer satisfaction ratings of its industry.

USAA follows the Golden Rule of customer support: Treat customers the way you would want to be treated if you were a customer. Not surprisingly, USAA has never been the victim of an online attack. Although customers occasionally post gripes about individual incidents, others policy-holders quickly rally to USAA's defense. That's the best way to defend against attack: Build a loyal customer base that heads off attacks before they begin.[1]

This chapter is based on Greg Gianforte's experience working with about 2,000 of the world's largest consumer brands and described in his book, *Eight to Great: Eight Steps to Delivering an Exceptional Customer Experience*. We've updated his recommendations and added examples of how organizations are using new channels to build loyal and enthusiastic followings.

When a company builds a comprehensive plan that continually exceeds in customer expectations, intense loyalty develops, and that's the best defense against attacks. Loyal customers give a company the benefit of the doubt when a problem occurs and are more likely to reach out to the business first instead of attacking it on Twitter or Facebook.

Let's first define what we mean by customer experience and explore why it's becoming more critical.

Customer experience is the sum total of all interactions that customers have with a brand and the perceptions they form as a result. These include online interactions, dealings with retailers or channel partners, the out-of-the-box experience, the long-term user experience, post-sales support, maintenance and the brand's ability to anticipate and respond to future needs. Basically, it's everything under the brand's control that impacts customer perceptions.

Many interactions offer opportunities to learn more about the customer's needs and preferences and to strengthen the relationship. Failing to amass as much knowledge as you can about your market leads to missed new product opportunities and annoyed customers. On the flip side, good analytics helps you predict customer needs before they're even aware of them.

We'd argue that customer experience is one of the few remaining sources of sustainable competitive advantage. You need good products, of course, but innovative products are quickly knocked off by competitors these days. Competing on price is a riskier strategy than ever because off-shore competitors drive margins out of the business.

Customer experience is impossible to knock off cheaply, and it's also one of the most potent marketing tools businesses have at their disposal. No one pays attention to advertising any more unless the ads are remarkable or entertaining. Word-of-mouth marketing is the new advertising. Raving fans who talk and tweet about the businesses they love are the kind of credible endorsements that no marketing spend can match.

Loyalty on the Wane

Have you heard of "showrooming?" That's a new term for the phenomenon in which customers walk the floors of a retail store scanning bar codes with their smart phones and looking up competitive prices online. Showrooming is killing the electronics retailing business, and it will only become a bigger problem as the quality and speed of mobile technology improves. Customer loyalty has been declining for years, and businesses in commodity markets are facing a world of hurt.

Customers have more choice than ever, which means they have fewer reasons than ever to do business with brands that don't provide exceptional experiences. Accenture reported that 66% of global consumers switched providers in at least one industry in 2011 due to poor customer service, up from 59% in 2009.[2] Customers are also less patient than ever. A ClickFox survey of 427 U.S. consumers found that nearly half said the most critical time to capture their loyalty is at the time of their first purchase.[3] In other words, you only have one chance to delight customers, and if you anger them they don't hesitate to make their grips public.

Some retail businesses are fighting back successfully by transforming the point-of-sale experience. Barnes & Noble has so far survived brutal online competition by transforming its bookstores into reading rooms. ING Direct used a similar strategy to remodel bank lobbies into coffee shops. Ikea makes furniture shopping a family outing. So does Jordan's Furniture, a New England retailer that has effectively transformed its stores into amusement parks.

Customer expectations are rising as businesses leapfrog each other with service innovations. Customer service has become an arms race, and success comes from knowing exactly who your customers are and what motivates them. Psychographics has succeeded demographics as the gold standard of customer segmentation.

These mega-trends of socially empowered consumers, fewer means of sustainable differentiation, declining marketing effectiveness, expanded customer choice and rising expectations are a mandate for a comprehensive customer experience strategy. What choice do you have?

Recent research has validated that service now outranks quality and price as the most important factor in customer loyalty. As we mentioned in Chapter 1, people are willing to pay a premium for great service. As a result, customer experience investments typically pay for themselves in higher margins, lower customer attrition and repeat business.

Temkin Group has estimated that a $1 billion company can generate more than $300 million over three years with a modest improvement in customer experience.[4] The research firm further estimated that many companies have evolved to a new level of customer experience awareness, one in which best practices are codified and embedded in the organization. Its study found that 59% of large companies aspire to be industry leaders in customer experience within three years.

Many Have Failed

They have a long way to go. The American Customer Satisfaction Index (ACSI) has documented only slight improvements in overall customer satisfaction since the score hit a low in 1997. It wasn't until 2008 that the National ACSI returned to the 1994 baseline levels (see chart).[5]

A late-2011 survey of 200 British customers and customer service professionals by Henley Business School and CDC Software found that 75% of consumers said customer service standards in the UK were at an all-time low and 62% feel no loyalty to the companies they do business with because they feel under-valued.[6]

RightNow Technologies' research has consistently found that only about 1% of consumers believe their experience expectations are always met.[7] How can this be, given the billions of dollars that companies have spent on customer relationship management (CRM) software?

One reason is that customers don't want to be managed. They want to be served. But that's not how CRM has traditionally been sold. CRM's roots are in sales force automation, an inwardly focused process automation discipline that aims to optimize sales productivity. Customer experience has nothing to do with it.

Real CRM looks at the business from the customer's perspective with the assumption that happy customers spend more, cost less

Source: American Customer Satisfaction Index

and tell others about their experience. Unfortunately, those benefits are tougher to measure than dollars-per-sales-rep. Most companies buy CRM for the wrong reason.

What's important isn't to manage customers, it's to let customer manage *you*.

Another problem with traditional CRM projects is that they tend to support managers rather than frontline employees. The idea is to optimize efficiency by standardizing customer interactions. The problem with that approach is that it sacrifices the flexibility frontline employees need to deal with customers as individuals. As we noted in Chapter 4, the most common source of attack is a single customer's negative experience. We have nothing against policies, but they need to be structured around customer needs, not management reports.

Having a comprehensive customer experience strategy is the key to survival in today's tumultuous business climate, but it's a huge undertaking. The rest of this chapter introduces an incremental eight-step process that has been used by thousands of companies around the world to build comprehensive customer experience strategies. We call it Eight to Great.

Eight Steps to Great Customer Experience

Start by finding the areas where improvements can be most quickly made. That means assessing your organization's strengths and weaknesses.

The reality is that few organizations really understand the experience they provide. One survey found that 80% of companies believed they delivered a "superior" customer experience but only 8% of customers agreed. Talk about a disconnect!

Avoid the Pitfalls

Because the customer experience is influenced by many types of interactions across many touch points, companies often make the mistake of defining their initial projects too broadly. Start with the stuff that delivers quantifiable, near-term results that justify continued investment.

Another frequent error is to approach the process in terms of what *you want* customers to do instead of *what customers want*. That's backwards.

A third common mistake is to over-rely on technology or process change to bring about improvements. Tools don't solve anything. They merely support changes that have to be internalized across the organization, starting at the top.

The following guidelines should help you avoid those common pitfalls.

- **Take a staged, incremental approach**. Look for quick-hit improvements that deliver the kind of near-term results that build credibility with decision-makers.

- **Adhere rigorously to the customer's perspective.** Improvements to the customer experience begin with focusing on customer wants and needs. This may call for changes in both business processes and organizational structure. Be aware of this possibility and get the support of one or more executives who can help make change happen.

- **Adopt the right technologies along with proven best practices.** While we don't recommend starting with technology, it can sometimes include best practices that prevent mistakes. Enterprise resource planning software transformed many large businesses in the late 1990s because it imposed discipline on processes that were ad hoc at many companies. Look for technology partners that support the changes you want to make.

- **Maintain a proactive — rather than a reactive — mindset.** You need to create a culture that fosters behaviors that create outstanding customer experiences. These include answering questions before they're asked, anticipating problems before they happen and personalizing interactions based on previous experience.

The Customer Experience Scorecard

The Customer Experience Scorecard (Table 2) helps quantify your organization's current customer experience and highlight areas that most need improvement. We've included sample scores from a fictitious company to show how the tool can be applied. Your results will obviously differ.

You can apply the following eight steps to successfully differentiate your company's customer experience:

1.   Establish a knowledge foundation;

2.   Empower customers with self-service;

3.   Empower frontline staff;

4.   Offer multichannel choice;

5.   Listen to your customers;

Table 2:

Customer Experience Scorecard	Strongly Agree:5	Agree:4	Neutral:3	Disagree:2	Strongly Disagree:1	Score
We know immediately if there is an issue brewing in social media channels and have social-savvy staff ready to engage.			X			3
Our customers are empowered to help themselves when they need information from us.		X				4
Customers can conveniently contact us via the channel of their choice (voice, e-mail, online, chat).			X			3
Regardless of how customers contact us, they will receive the same answer to the same question.			X			3
When a customer calls, we know whether he or she has recently been contacted by us.			X			3
Customers can track and view their interactions (order history, account status).		X				4
Our employees have a single view of all customer interactions regardless of type.			X			3

When we engage with our customers, we provide them with relevant, personalized information.	X					5
We capture the voice of the customer by proactively seeking feedback, and we take immediate action when necessary.			X			3
We continually exceed our service goals (first-call resolution rate, service-level agreements).				X		2
We help connect our customers with one another by offering events, communities, or forums.					X	1
TOTAL						34

40–50: Ready to implement strategies for continual improvement

30–39: Targeted improvements required

0–29: Broad improvements required

6. Design seamless experiences;

7. Engage proactively with customers; and

8. Measure and improve continually.

The following sections build on these eight steps to provide a plan that yields dramatic results.

Step 1: Establish a Knowledge Foundation

Have you ever contacted a company and talked with a friendly representative who was no help at all? The rep didn't know your order history or account balance and couldn't answer basic questions about product features, return policies or warranties. The only assistance he or she could offer was to transfer you to someone else.

This type of experience is far too common. These interactions frustrate customers and are also costly for companies because poor service leads to customer defections. Fortunately, the solution is straightforward: Provide the right knowledge to the right person at the right time. Because lack of knowledge is at the root of many negative customer experiences, the first step in delivering an exceptional customer experience is establishing a knowledge foundation.

A knowledge foundation should be easily accessible by employees and customers alike. Employees can use it as a source of information to enhance customer interactions. Customers use it for self-service and to speed online interactions with your company.

Your knowledge foundation should contain two primary types of knowledge:

- Knowledge about your products, services and company. Think of this as answers to your customers' most likely questions.

- Knowledge about your customers. Examples include demographics, past purchases, interaction history and explicit and implicit preferences.

Building a Knowledge Foundation

Establishing a knowledge foundation doesn't need to consume a lot of resources. Don't even try to build one manually. It's time-consuming, expensive, inflexible and quickly outdated. Manual methods also typically reflect what subject matter experts believe is important, rather than what customers need.

A better approach is to create a framework that enables customers and employees to build the foundation as a byproduct of their daily work.

Consider the breakthrough approaches of eBay and YouTube. Conventional wisdom would have directed eBay employees to monitor sellers' auctions and provide post-sale service, but eBay instead lets buyers rank and review the quality of sellers' merchandise and service. Amazon does the same thing with its customer reviews.

Likewise, YouTube could have hired people to view submissions to ensure quality control and rank them according to their personal preferences, but it instead invented a self-regulating approach in which views, likes and comments determine a video's search ranking. That was a good strategy, since at last report YouTube was logging 72 hours of video uploads every *minute*. Both companies scaled their businesses because they let their customers decide how to manage the product.

Today, there are technologies that can be used behind the firewall to enable employees to share ideas and practices that delight customers. These internal social networks bypass traditional hierarchies and let people connect directly with their peers.

For example, when TD Bank North used its private social network to ask employees about their biggest frustrations, one teller suggested that a paper-based enrollment process could be handled more efficiently online. Her comment drew endorsements from hundreds of other employees and led to the "biggest single productivity improvement of the year," according to Wendy Arnott, vice president of social media and digital communications.[8] Companies like Caterpillar, Inc. and Xerox Corp. are embracing these technologies because they unlock knowledge of the people who are closest to the front lines.

You probably have thousands of customers interacting with you daily through your website, e-mail, chat and the phone. Let them suggest content and assess quality. This approach, combined with the right self-learning technology, will assure that your knowledge foundation is what your customers want, is always up to date and dynamically adjusts to changing customer needs.

How to Build a Knowledge Foundation

Once you've selected a knowledge base technology, it's straightforward to build a knowledge foundation.

- **Seed.** Quickly establish your knowledge foundation by seeding it with a limited number of questions and answers. Don't try to load the kitchen sink. Start with basic information, and add content over time. A good way to determine what information you need is to spend an afternoon in your contact center listening to agents. You'll find that they spend most time answering basic questions. Use those questions and answers as the starting point for your knowledge foundation. You'll quickly discover that a small amount of information addresses a wide range of customer inquiries and needs. Seed your initial knowledge foundation with 30 (or fewer) question-and-answer pairs, which can take the form of an FAQ list. You can add more later.

- **Capture**. Use the self-learning capabilities of your system to determine where gaps exist in your knowledge foundation, based on actual customer interactions. Every question that is submitted via your website or via e-mail points to potential information gaps. Capture your people's responses to these questions, and route them for possible approval and publishing.

- **Organize**. Businesses tend to organize knowledge based on attributes such as products and locations. Customers, however, often think in terms of product uses or types of problems. Organizing information for easy access is the most critical step in building your knowledge foundation. Good software tools automatically learn from the information entered into them and float the most likely answers to the top. This can make the customer self-service process a lot easier. For example, when Nikon Corp. implemented a self-learning system for consumer self-service, inbound e-mail and phone calls dropped by 50% as customers found immediate answers online.

Deliver to the Front Lines

A knowledge system in isolation is like Einstein's brain without a body: smart, but of little use. To drive business value, your knowledge foundation must connect directly to the business applications across all the customer touch channels in your business (e-mail, Web, phone, interactive voice response, agent desktop, social media and chat). It must also be visible to search engines because that's where customers are going to look.

Rather than overhauling your company's IT environment, implement an open knowledge foundation that can leverage a full range of data sources, including CRM databases, return merchandise authorization systems, Web content, transaction processing systems, online bulletin boards, business intelligence applications and other relevant information resources. Make the tool available to anyone who interacts with the customer. Don't keep customer insight private.

Step 2: Empower Customers with Self-Service

One of the most powerful — and immediately rewarding — ways to improve the customer experience is to expose your knowledge foundation to customers through effective self-service mechanisms. By giving customers easy, direct access to your knowledge foundation, you enable them to find the information they need whenever they want it.

This may seem counter-intuitive. After all, isn't great customer service all about personal interaction? Not necessarily. Customers actually appreciate the speed, convenience and control of taking care of their own needs. Self-service options not only significantly improve cost-efficiency but actually contribute to customer satisfaction. A 2012 NCR survey of supermarket shoppers found that 64% agreed with the statement, "I believe retailers who offer self checkout provide better customer service."[9]

When customers choose self-service options, call volumes decrease, giving agents more time for complex questions and personalized service, which enhances the customer experience and reduces costs. RightNow Technologies deployed thousands of Web self-service portals and often saw self-services rates (the percentage of visitors who found an answer online and didn't have to call) of well over 90%. Immediate reductions of 30% to 50% in inbound customer e-mail and call center reductions of 5% to 20% were also common.

Additional benefits of self-service, for both customers and your company, can include:

- **Speed** — Self-service enables customers to find information immediately without waiting for an e-mail response or for a call center agent.

- **Round-the-clock service** — Organizations that can't afford to operate a 24-hour contact center can let consumers find help during off hours.

- **Effectiveness** — Diagrams, photos, and video clips are often more effective demonstration tools than phone interactions. Be sure to optimize titles for search so customers can find them easily.

- **Relief for other channels** — An effective self-service environment can reduce the workloads of agents, employees and partners who assist customers, and it can enable them to spend more time with customers who require personal attention — which can lead to dramatic improvements in the overall customer experience.

- **True first-contact resolution** — Many consumers check websites for answers before contacting a company. By providing Web self-service, companies can ensure that customers get what they need quickly.

Staffing the contact center to deal with sudden peaks in demand can be costly and impractical. Web and voice self-service, in comparison, can scale to handle large numbers of interactions without additional staff. Online communities, where customers can chat with one another directly, have also emerged as an effective self-service technique. These can be implemented on a website using commercial or open source software applications, or even provided in a public forum like Facebook. One customer in National Instruments' LabVIEW support community has answered more than 15,000 questions since 1999. Imagine how much money that has saved National Instruments.

Encouraging Customers to Use Self-Service

When promoting self-service channels, be sure to offer customers a range of choices for interaction, and don't forget to include ways for customers to quickly escalate issues or reach live support. Any of the following methods can help to drive certain customer interactions to lower-cost, self-service channels:

- Make online self-service links prominent on your website, and always offer self-service options first or at the same time that you offer a customer support phone number or e-mail address.

- Integrate online help throughout key processes, such as purchases or returns.

- Promote Web and voice self-service resources in the messages customers hear while on hold.

- Have call center agents notify customers of self-service options, and, if needed, provide instructions on how to use them.

- Accept questions from customers via Web forms that can also be used to suggest appropriate self-service content.

- Reply to e-mail with a hyperlink to appropriate self-service content, instead of providing a complete answer by e-mail. This reinforces the fact that self-service is available.

Measuring Self-Service Effectiveness

To gauge the effectiveness of self-service options, you need to determine self-service rates. Track the total number of Web and phone self-service sessions on your site and compare this with the number of visitors who escalate issues to the contact center by calling, sending e-mail, using a Web form or initiating a chat session. Many organizations have achieved Web self-service rates of 90%, and some have achieved rates as high as 99% when most customer inquiries are routine.

About 80% of contact centers have implemented some kind of customer self-service, but many still don't understand its effectiveness. A 2010 survey of 400 contact center pros by the International Customer Management Institute found that 64% didn't know when customers had tried a self-serve option first but then opted for a live representative and 43% didn't measure customer feedback on their self-service channels.[10] Knowing these basic metrics is critical to understanding whether your self-service options are pleasing or frustrating the customer.

Step 3: Empower Frontline Staff

You can't stop with self-service, however, because much of your customer experience may involve interactions between customers and your people on the front lines. You must fully empower employees to exceed customer expectations. The payoff from even a single interaction can be enormous.

For example, Paul has bought all his appliances from one local retailer for years because of a single telephone interaction. Paul called the company to dispatch a repairman to fix a dryer that wasn't dry-ing. Expecting to write a check for hundreds of dollars, he was stunned when the merchant instead guided him through the process of fixing the dryer himself. The retailer hadn't even sold him the dryer in the first place.

Paul has since spent more than $10,000 with the small company and even wrote its first Yelp review. Many other people have since added their own five-star ratings, resulting in a steady stream of new business for the three-person operation. That's the power of delighting one customer.

By giving frontline employees the means to go above and beyond the basics of customer support, you create the potential to create raving fans. Make information available about customers' previous interactions so that employees can personalize conversation, show that they understand the customers' needs and save repetition and frustration.

Other ways to empower frontline staff with the knowledge needed to deliver a great customer experience include the following:

- **Interview veterans**. Experienced frontline employees are typically familiar with the most common customer requests. They're great training resources. Veterans can also tell you which policies irritate both customers and agents.

  Veteran employees sometimes resist so-called "knowledge capture" efforts because they see it as a threat to their job. Rather than using an awkward question-and-answer format, invite veterans to teach classes or mentor new employees. Internal social networks have also proven successful in coaxing veterans to share knowledge because they see the immediate impact of their advice on colleagues and customers.

- **Enable employees to update the knowledge foundation.** Employees can share and edit each other's experiences, and the knowledge base comes to represent the wisdom of the crowd.

- **Support them with technology.** How many times have your customer service interactions been slowed by poor network performance or sluggish software? Make sure the frontline staff has speedy workstations and software that quickly pulls up the information they need.

- **Continue to adapt.** Adjust knowledge resources to mirror changes in your business, such as seasonal information or new product details. Make it easy to escalate problems to subject matter gurus with minimal interruption.

- **Value your employees.** When people have to jump through hoops to get a day off or submit to video surveillance while working, they don't develop much loyalty. On the other hand, when companies treat employees with respect, people stay longer and encourage others to work there. What makes retailers like Trader Joe's, Costco and Nordstrom remarkable "is that they have a different labor model. Staff and customer service are not a cost; staff is an asset you invest in," says Marshall Fisher, a professor at the University of Pennsylvania's Wharton School.[11]

What You Measure Matters

If your telesales or customer support operation is measured by call duration and interactions-per-agent, you have no chance of delighting customers. These industrial-age metrics have no place in the service economy. Organizations that are committed to great customer experience measure attitudes, not time clocks. Send an e-mail survey to each customer following an interaction. If you keep these surveys short (not more than three questions), response rates can be surprisingly high, often above 35%. Ask for ratings on a numeric scale and always leave a space for detailed feedback. Many online survey tools support "conditional branching," which enables you to ask for more specifics if a customer expresses a strongly negative opinion. Some even offer the option to break out of a survey to speak to a representative.

We also recommend you conduct annual or semi-annual customer satisfaction surveys to detect changes over time. Not only do these vehicles give you insight on how customers rate your performance, they also deliver a wealth of insight for continual improvement. We discuss this in more detail in Step 5.

Step 4: Offer Multichannel Choice

When interacting with organizations, today's customers expect to have a range of options: phone, e-mail, website, chat, Facebook, Twitter, online communities, fax, traditional mail and in-person. Because many customers use these platforms interchangeably, they should be integrated to document a single, unified dialogue with each customer.

Follow the "Bouncing Customer"

Customers often jump from channel to channel in the course of a single incident. For example, a customer may e-mail a question and follow up with a phone call if a reply doesn't fully address an issue.

These calls can be especially frustrating for customers if agents don't have immediate access to information about customers' previous interactions with the organization.

To deliver consistently excellent customer experiences while offering customers a choice of communication channels, all customer interactions must be unified.

Everyone interacting with customers should be able to see all relevant previous exchanges with each customer, regardless of which channels were used. Unified channel management also eliminates redundancies that result when customers contact you with the same request via multiple channels.

By leveraging a common knowledge foundation across all communication channels, you can ensure that your organization provides customers with consistent information regardless of how you interact with them. A common knowledge foundation can also help to ensure that information shared with customers has been vetted by legal staff, compliance teams and corporate communications departments, if required. It also makes consolidated reporting a lot easier.

Optimize the Multichannel Experience

As you optimize your use of multiple channels, keep the following principles in mind.

- **Avoid the dead-end channel.** If customers have trouble finding what they need through one channel, they should be able to quickly switch to another. Without these options, customers may become frustrated and disinclined to use self-service again.

  We're amazed that so many companies provide no easy way for customers to exit their automated voice response systems and talk to a representative directly. These companies have their priorities wrong; they're putting process efficiency ahead of customer satisfaction. Sites like GetHuman.com, which document ways to get around voice response menus, shouldn't have to exist.

- **Provide a channel for customers to connect with one another.** Online communities can foster a sense of community and tap into the collective expertise of customers. They can also save a ton of money when customers help each other solve problems.

If you have a sizable customer base, it's likely that a customer community will develop around your products or services whether you're involved or not. By running your own customer community, you can respond to complaints in a controlled environment, get quick feedback from customers and cut support costs. You can also make information from these channels available to your own support staff. For example, the help system in Microsoft Office mixes content from bloggers and independent troubleshooting sites with Microsoft's own knowledge base. What a smart way to leverage the wisdom of the crowd!

Create Conferences and Events

Another way to strengthen customer relationships — particularly for B2B companies — is to bring people together physically. Events like regional meetings or "birds of a feather" gatherings at industry trade shows enable customers to share successes and challenges while also building brand loyalty. You don't need to spend a lot of money. You can usually rent a hotel conference room or restaurant function room for the price of some food and drink.

Twitter is a useful channel to create ad hoc events called "tweetups." These are informal meetings organized by hash tag, often in conjunction with an industry event. They are particularly popular with small companies that don't have the means to host a conference.

Choose a location like a bar or restaurant, reserve some space and start spreading the message of when and where to meet via Twitter. Choose a theme if appropriate. Encourage followers to re-tweet the details. It's a good idea to create a landing page or use a free service such as Eventbrite, Twitvite.com or Facebook Events to keep track of who plans to attend. You should probably spring for a round or two of drinks and some appetizers, but the cost is modest.

Don't Overdo It

Be sure that the communication channels you have in place are doing the job before launching news ones. Don't dive headlong into Facebook or Twitter support unless you have the staff and tools to do it right. If you can't respond to people within 24 hours, you're just going to create new problems for yourself.

That said, you should also be aware that customers increasingly are demanding that you use the channels *they* prefer. A poll of 4,000 U.K. consumers found that 65% of those who have used social media for customer support prefer it to traditional call centers.[12] Gartner has estimated that organizations that *don't* communicate with customers via social media could experience annual customer churn rates of up to 15% by 2014.[13]

Step 5: Listen to Your Customers

Delivering a consistently excellent customer experience is impossible if you don't have a systematic way to listen. You must understand customers' opinions on everything from the quality of your products to the helpfulness of your website. Effective listening sharpens your focus, weeds out unpopular products and enables you to correct problems before they escalate into crises.

As we outlined in Chapter 9, you should have a person or team of people who know and understand social media etiquette and are tasked with plugging into the networks where your customers and prospective customers gather. They should be listening for your products and service trademarks, but also for those of your competitors, market categories and related issues of interest.

In addition, clear rules of engagement should be defined. If a crisis is uncovered, what authority do your people have to speak on behalf of the company? How do they escalate the issue? Answers to those questions should be spelled out in a customer service handbook and in your company's social media policy.

Listening At the "Moment Of Truth"

Discovering that a customer is dissatisfied about an incident that occurred six months ago doesn't give you much to work with. The customer may have already gone elsewhere. Yet many companies survey customers only once or twice a year.

You should be aware of anything that may threaten a relationship at the time of the interaction, or the "moment of truth." Ask customers for feedback during or immediately after interactions, and make it easy for them to respond. As we noted earlier, feedback requests at the moment of truth can generate response rates of 35% or more, particularly when brief or tied to a coupon or other incentive. If you've got a problem, you want to know about it while the customer can still be saved.

There are software programs that perform "sentiment analysis" to detect emotional content in written comments. While the technology has its flaws, it's reasonably good at identifying extreme dissatisfaction. Twitter search even has an option to monitor posts for sentiment. While we don't believe every gripe deserves a response, a pattern of frustration demands attention.

Complement your "moment of truth" research with regular, broad-based customer satisfaction research or standardized metrics like Net Promoter Score.[14] This helps you detect changes in sentiment over time, and marketers and development teams can use this research to help in product design and promotion.

As your organization collects more detailed information about customers, you'll be able to target surveys based on multiple customer attributes. You'll also learn to execute surveys across channels using e-mail, Web, chat and automated voice systems.

Accentuate the Negative

As we've shown in case studies throughout this book, complaints are something to be embraced. Not only do negative comments offer the opportunity for improvement, but a small number of customers can now adversely influence many others. Public complaints are often just the tip of the iceberg.

One note of caution: Don't let high customer satisfaction scores make you complacent. They simply set a higher standard to maintain. As we noted in Chapter 7, getting to the top of the list on TripAdvisor means you have to work even harder to stay there.

Rapid responses to customer problems can strengthen relationships and increase loyalty. You need to capture customer feedback in real time, act on that feedback immediately and demonstrate how that feedback has changed the way you do business. Don't expect customers to figure this out for themselves. You need to tell them specifically how their feedback drives action. If you aren't going to use feedback to improve the customer experience, don't bother asking for it.

The following steps help to ensure that captured feedback is used to correct problems and improve performance:

- Automatically route negative feedback to the appropriate individual or department for fast action. Require that the person responsible contact the customer within a certain number of hours, as Wyndham Wingate's Scott Wright does. Make people accountable for taking action.

- Send a weekly report of all product-related complaints to product and manufacturing managers, along with the steps you took to resolve them.

- Analyze, summarize or aggregate feedback so others can spot trends, take appropriate action and learn appropriate response strategies. The more you do this, the more adept you will become at resolving issues.

- Report feedback trends to executive management on a scheduled basis.

Be sure to track complaints through to final resolution. An engagement shouldn't be closed out of your CRM system until the customer can be classified as satisfied or the problem is beyond resolution. Not all problems can be resolved to everyone's satisfaction, so have limits in place. For example, a complaint might be classified as unresolvable after three attempts to contact the customer with no response.

When multiple complaints arise about the same issue, have an escalation process in place. You might have a product defect problem on your hands. Support staff should be notified immediately if a recall is merited or a product is being pulled from the market. All this information should also be in your knowledge foundation.

When customers provide feedback, close the loop. Thank them, and let them know what you're doing with the information they gave you. Asking for feedback and then ignoring it is worse than not asking for feedback at all.

Employees must know that customer feedback is highly valued. Tying compensation to satisfaction scores is an obvious tactic, but not all rewards have to be financial. Celebrate improvements in satisfaction rankings in newsletters, company meetings or stockholder briefings. Positive satisfaction rankings are also great fodder for public relations, advertising, and branding campaigns.

Consider an Ideation Community

Online ideation communities are essentially focus groups where customers can contribute ideas and vote on one another's contributions. Examples include Dell's Ideastorm, MyStarbucks Idea and Bed Bath & Beyond's Quirky.

Companies that host such communities find that the best ideas quickly float to the top and that customers take pride in having direct impact on products and policies. B2B companies have found particular value in ideation communities. For example, software giant SAP has more than 2 million customers and partners registered in its communities. National Instruments gets many of its best product enhancement ideas directly from customers in this way.

Ideation communities don't have to be as technically sophisticated as the ones mentioned above. A basic threaded discussion group can do the trick.

For example, the Ridge Tool Company's RIDGID Forum has more than 37,000 members, most of them plumbers, electricians and HVAC professionals. The community provides a constant stream of product evaluations, ideas and feedback to the company. It's also a great source of word-of-mouth marketing. RIDGID Forum runs on vBulletin, a community platform that costs just a few hundred dollars.

Step 6: Design Seamless Experiences

If you've ever contacted a company to ask about a special offer you received in the mail and found that the agent knew nothing about the offer, or if you've received a sales call from a company that won't return your support calls, you've experienced the negative effects of a "siloed" organization. In many organizations, multiple teams interact with customers, yet they don't work with one another. Acquisitions, software incompatibilities or simple lack of good management control creates a bad experience for customers.

To break down operational walls, consider your organization from the customer's perspective. Try doing business anonymously with your own company and evaluate the experience. Who do customers deal with at each stage of the transaction? How does service delivery match your expectations? How much information do you have to provide to get an answer, and do you have to provide it several times? Understanding the gaps in service is the first step toward designing a seamless customer experience.

Designing for the Customer

As you design cross-departmental processes and workflows, consider how these can be automated with software. Automating multistep customer interactions ensures a seamless experience, even when multiple handoffs are involved. Be sure that anyone who interacts with customers can easily escalate issues to others. For example, encourage contact center staff to alert field support of recurring problems. Senior management should explicitly state that negative feedback from customers and frontline staff is welcomed and not punished. Customers with critical feedback should also be encouraged to suggest solutions and rewarded with thanks and even small incentives. These guidelines will help you streamline workflows.

- **Build rich customer profiles**. Frontline staff should be able to review and/or modify attributes in customer records, such as noting which products a customer uses, changing an address or adding details that can be used to personalize future interactions. All customer attributes should be current, accurate and easily accessible by anyone who works with customers.

- **Use this information to provide specialized attention**, such as discounts based on past purchases. We know of

196

one cable company whose voice response system tells every caller, "We see that you're one of our most valued customers." How disingenuous is that? If everyone is special, then no one is special. What if the company instead offered a free pay-per-view movie to customers who had purchased more than three movies during the past month? It's not that hard to put this kind of information in the hands of customer support people or even automated response systems.

- **Make workflow rules flexible**. Authorized managers should be able to create and modify workflow rules, such as yes/no decision trees and event triggers, based upon customer feedback. For example, if hold times are a problem, route the customer to an automated attendant that can call the customer back when the backlog eases. Managers on the front lines should be the ones who determine these thresholds.

Giving managers the ability to implement and change workflow rules without the help of technical staff is essential. If you use customer support software, make sure your vendor provides this kind of functionality or makes it a priority enhancement.

- **Move as much support online as possible**. Customers' preference for online self-service has been thoroughly documented, so give people what they want. Offer chat support, FAQs, how-to videos and Web forms. If you promise e-mail response, deliver within 24 hours.

- **Give nontechnical staff tools that allow them to post and remove Web content**, such as technical alerts or time-sensitive promotions, without the assistance of IT. Your organization must be able to change online content quickly in response to changing market dynamics, actions of competitors or other conditions.

- **Automate certain customer communications**. For example, during peak buying seasons, customers may appreciate knowing about free shipping offers. You can notify customers that service contracts should be renewed, that

197

account payments are overdue or that new product models are available. Social media offers unprecedented new ways to communicate this information, and you should use every channel your customers use.

Step 7: Engage Proactively with Customers

Many companies take the "emergency room" approach to dealing with customers. They wait until the "patient" is brought in on a stretcher and then practice triage. Little consideration is given to what caused the problem; the focus is on fixing it and sending the patient away. However, any health professional will tell you that success is keeping patients out of the emergency room in the first place.

Your goal should be to address the factors that erode customer satisfaction the most. By understanding your customers and their history with your company, you can move your customer experience from the emergency room to the fitness center.

Key Principles of Effective Customer Communications

When communicating with customers, keep the following principles in mind:

- **Segmentation**. Information should be delivered only to customers for whom it is relevant. Relevance should be based on customer attributes, such as the location or purchase history.

  Relevance is particularly important in e-mail communications because customers who receive irrelevant messages may opt out or ignore future messages. Don't over-communicate. Unless customers have specifically requested it, limit proactive communications to twice a month.

A combination of a knowledge foundation and the appropriate analytical tools can help you narrow down communications only to those that are most relevant to each customer. Once you've segmented customers, determine how to proactively engage with each segment in the most appropriate manner. For example, middle-aged men should get different promotions than young mothers. Travel companies might alert customers of summer vacation specials during spring months and online retailers can promote free shipping near the holidays. Frequent or loyal customers should get different offers than one-time visitors.

- **Personalization**. Always respond to the recipient by name rather than with a generic greeting. Communications should reflect knowledge of specific interactions with each customer. For example, if a new accessory is available for a certain product, notify only those customers who have purchased that product.

- **Authenticity**. If frontline staff members convey during each interaction that they're passionate about helping customers, then customers will come to believe them. That takes training.

  The same goes for your social media presence. While there's nothing wrong with speaking to customers through branded accounts, you'll get a warmer reception when a human being does the talking. Even a person speaking through a branded account can use a conversational tone to make the interaction more personal.

Campaign management software, which is built into many CRM suites or offered as an add-on, helps create intelligent, multichannel event-triggered campaigns that push information to customers through the right channel at the right time.

Step 8: Measure and Improve Continually

The seven steps previously described are the foundation of a great customer experience, but success is a process, not an event. You must continually measure your performance and foster a culture that drives continual improvement.

Keep the Ball Rolling

Because you'll be constantly compared to your competition, pay special attention to those competitors that are recognized for best-in-class service. Many organizations and media outlets reward the best of the best. Study the winners. There's nothing wrong with copying great ideas.

Use case studies like those described in earlier chapters to create a "what not to do" primer for the organization. Subscribe to The Consumerist's RSS feed or the Consumer Warning Network[15] to keep current. Monitor the #fail hash tag on Twitter.

- **Monitor competitors.** Always watch what other companies in your industry are doing. Become their customer and experience how they interact with you. What do they do differently that you could learn from?

- **Network with peers.** Many technology vendors provide opportunities through local user groups, seminars and conferences. Attend at least one conference focused on the customer experience each year. Keep an eye out for educational sessions on this topic or take the initiative to form your own peer group. Meetup.com is an easy and inexpensive way to create local groups around any topic you can imagine.

- **Take advantage of tune-ups.** Your CRM or call center technology providers should offer free best-practice consultations at least twice annually. During these tune-ups, the vendor should review the quality of your customer experience and make recommendations for improvement. If your vendor doesn't offer this kind of service, ask for it or consider taking your business elsewhere.

- **Hire the pros.** A professional services organization with customer experience expertise can be brought in to do a limited-scope discovery engagement. This includes observing contact center agents at work, reviewing your website and interviewing internal stakeholders. The results should include a list of recommended, prioritized customer experience projects, as well as a comparison of your organization's customer experience with industry best practices.

- **Aim for incremental improvements.** Try implementing one improvement each quarter. Assess whether the changes are moving the customer satisfaction needle. Double down on your winners, and fold your losers.

Measure Performance

The Customer Experience Scorecard from earlier in this chapter suggests assessment criteria you can use to measure progress. You should review these continually, but don't go overboard. Many organizations track too many metrics when just a few are true indicators of customer experience quality. Here's a short list to consider.

- **Customer satisfaction and Net Promoter Score** are two of the more popular high-level customer experience metrics. Customer satisfaction surveys measure recent transactions, while Net Promoter Score, which we described earlier in this chapter, is a better indicator of satisfaction over time.

- **Up-sell/cross-sell rates** gauge the success of follow-on revenue. Improvements in these areas are usually a direct result of quality customer interactions.

- **Conversion rate** refers to the percentage of new customer interactions that turn into a sale. While typically applied to marketing and sales engagements, conversion rates can also be applied to call center or customer community interactions.

For example, Care One, a provider of debt-relief services, uses an informational online community to generate leads. The company tracks sources of new business and has found that people who engage with the community before filling out a lead form are nearly four times as likely to sign up for a debt-relief plan and more than three times as likely to make the first payment. The company essentially uses customer support to generate new business.

One note of caution on using traditional contact center performance metrics: They can be misleading. For example, the popular First Call Resolution Rate (FCRR) metric doesn't take into account the likelihood that by the time customers call or e-mail a company, they've probably already visited a website, bounced around a phone system, spoken with a store employee or been confused by instructions in a product manual. What many companies view as FCRR is actually second contact resolution rate. To measure true FCRR, you must determine that the call center is really the first interaction.

The ultimate goal of any customer experience initiative should be a high Zero Contact Resolution Rate. That metric indicates that you understand customers well enough to anticipate their needs. The only way to measure that it is to ask customers if they have ever sought trouble-shooting help of any kind. If you can increase that percentage, you're doing well.

Guidelines for Using Customer Experience Metrics

In addition to measuring and monitoring your organization's performance, use metrics to drive actions and behaviors that continually improve the customer experience. The following best practices will help you get the most value out of your customer experience metrics.

- **Communicate your goals**. Everyone involved in your customer experience initiative should know which metrics have been defined as key performance indicators and why. For example, if you establish your self-service usage goal as 90%, communicate that to your team. Compensation should always be tied to specific and measurable goals.

- **Make your goals visible**. Desktop dashboards in call-center software make it easy for staff to monitor performance and track progress. You can also post signage to indicate progress.

- **Reward achievement.** Celebrate success with internal publicity, milestone awards and friendly competition. The size of the award is less important than the enthusiasm with which you present it.

The Final Step: Making It Happen

Transforming customer experience from adequate to outstanding requires deliberate, consistent action by many people. It also requires leadership; someone must have the vision to champion change and the skills to guide the organization to success.

If you are leading or involved in a customer experience initiative, keep the following guidelines in mind:

- **Take it step-by-step**. Because optimization of the customer experience can require extensive change across many parts of an organization, it can be tempting to launch a large project with lofty goals. Resist that temptation. Massive "boil-the-ocean" projects can overwhelm employees and drain budgets. Also, the greater the scope of your initiative, the more likely you are to encounter multiple pockets of resistance.

  A more effective approach is to focus on a specific area until you achieve the desired results. Producing near-term results helps to build credibility and gain support. Keep the long-term goal in mind, but look for short-term successes.

- **Do the right things in the right order.** The eight steps are listed in an order that has helped thousands of companies improve their customer experience. If you're not able to provide fast, accurate answers to customers' basic questions, then trying to up-sell to them doesn't make sense. Likewise, adding Twitter support when your basic e-mail and call center channels are weak won't improve your customer experience. Master each stage incrementally.

Most organizations implement the eight steps in the order described here, but you may need to apply them differently depending on your situation. What's most important is that they help you make customer experience a top priority.

Parting Shots

Back in 2007, Paul devoted one of his monthly columns in *BtoB* magazine to a Microsoft online experiment that seemed incredible at the time. The company had set up a blog called Port25 and invited critics from the open source software community to engage in a conversation.

To understand how ground-breaking this was, you need to know that Microsoft was considered the Great Satan by open source advocates at the time. Given an invitation to vent their hostility, thousands of critics gleefully flocked to Port25 to layer insults on their foe. Microsoft staffers responded with restraint and courtesy. They deleted only the most profane comments but let pretty much everything else stand. They posted reasoned responses that admitted to differences of opinion, but they also spotlighted evidence that Microsoft was genuinely committed to participate in the community. Over a few weeks, the conversation turned civil and even collegial at times. Microsoft may never be an ally of the open source movement, but it proved that engagement is more productive than indifference.[1]

It's hard to accept criticism cheerfully or to regard a complaint — in Barlow and Møller's words — as a gift. Yet the open, two-way dialogue between organizations and their constituents that has evolved with the arrival of social media is beginning to change old habits. We're convinced it's for the better.

We've been impressed, for example, by the way package delivery services such as UPS, Federal Express and DHL maintain their Facebook presences. These companies pull off millions of miracles each day. They ship packages thousands of miles in a few hours for just a few dollars. Forty years ago such a feat seemed impossible,[2] but the customers who flock to FedEx's Facebook page don't seem to be too impressed.

Rather, they come there to complain. They bitch about missed deliveries and damaged packages and surly drivers and unexpected surcharges and stuff that's delivered to the wrong address and everything else you can image. They do the same on the Facebook pages of DHL and UPS. All three services field these gripes with disarming cheerfulness. They know that vocal customers are offering them a chance to retain their loyalty and that a sympathetic ear and a can-do attitude show that a company really cares about their business. Why don't more businesses do this?

Corporations, government agencies and even nonprofit organizations have lived in a bubble for many years. They've either chosen not to hear about their mistakes or to keep such conversations behind closed doors. Now they have no choice. Their performance evaluations are being crafted every day by every customer they serve, and there isn't a thing they can do to change that. Today's markets mete out swift and brutal punishment to companies that don't meet customers' expectations. If you don't listen, you're road kill.

Once you can wrestle your mind away from regarding complaints as problems and learn to welcome them as opportunities, your whole organization changes. Employees stop playing defense and start taking initiative when they see that customer satisfaction trumps financial and operational goals. Ideas for improving the customer experience bubble up through the ranks. Managers stop punishing people for taking risks, which causes innovation to flourish. The whole organization becomes more focused, positive and creative. In our age of low switching costs, even lower brand loyalty and relentless global competition, is the importance of customer satisfaction even a debatable issue?

We still have a long way to go. As we were writing this concluding chapter, Paul had a travel experience with which all seasoned flyers can sympathize. Stuck in a remote airport for eight hours as equipment failures and canceled flights frustrated his efforts to get to a client meeting the next day, he finally succeeded in getting a spot on a red-eye flight that would put him into town 12 hours later than planned on three hours of sleep. After standing in line for nearly three hours, he begged the gate agent for one favor:

Could the airline grant him a seat with a little extra leg room so he could stretch out his 6'3" frame and sleep? "Sure," the agent replied, cheerfully. "That'll be $79."

That carrier was United Airlines. Perhaps Dave Carroll's video valentine hasn't yet percolated through the ranks.

We remain optimistic, though. The transparency that open customer dialogue demands will transform all but the most monopolistic organizations. It will either make them better or make them obsolete. Either way we'll be better off. For every United upgrade fee experience, we see five other examples of companies going above and beyond to delight us. And the ratio is improving.

Guy Kawasaki, the one-time Apple evangelist whose books and speeches have made him an ambassador for business excellence, preaches that great companies are those that enchant their customers. He challenges them to do something "DICEE." That stands for deep, intelligent, complete, empowering and elegant. Apple has been DICEE for years, but you don't have to be an industry icon to enchant your customers.

Enchantment can be accepting a return with no questions asked. It's the extra scoop of ice cream you give because you were out of the flavor the customer really wanted. It's delivering the package in three days when you committed to five. It's gift-wrapping the purchase because the buyer mentioned it was an anniversary present. It's cracking a joke to relieve a tense situation. It's letting the flight attendant deliver the safety rules in rap.

We love JetBlue Airways' latest ad campaign: "You Above All." The tagline "underscores our commitment to always put people first, to bring humanity back to air travel," said the company's senior marketing vice president. It's not surprising that JetBlue has topped all other low-cost carriers in J.D. Power and Associates' customer satisfaction research for seven years in a row.

You Above All. That isn't so hard, is it?

Acknowledgements

The hardest part of writing a book about this topic was finding people who would talk about their experiences as attack victims. I'm particularly grateful to Paul Fox and Stan Joosten of Procter & Gamble, who agreed to open the kimono on an incident that had caused considerable pain for the Pampers team two years earlier. I had the privilege of serving on P&G's Digital Advisory Board for three years and learned that this is no ordinary corporate giant. The commitment of its people and culture to understanding and satisfying customers is remarkable.

Other people who have been generous with their time and guidance include Michael Atkinson, Janelle Barlow, Richard Binhammer, Kristen Christian, David-Michel Davies, Sam Decker, Jenny Dervin, Frank Eliason, Rob Fuggetta, Bob Garfield, Jessica Gottlieb, Nick Hayes, Shel Holtz, Stephanie Ichinose, Scott Monty, Mike Moran, Mickey Nelson, Jeremiah Owyang, Katie Paine, Ben Popken, Jenny Barnett Rohrs, Rosana Shah and Steve Zenofsky. IBM's Leslie Reiser showed great tolerance for my erratic schedule as I mixed book-writing with my day job helping support her company's social marketing strategy. A special thanks to Shel Holtz and his colleague, Neville Hobson, for their weekly For Immediate Release podcast. I never miss an episode, and they are always up on the latest social media kerfuffle.

Pete Blackshaw made an earnest effort to connect from his new post at Nestlé in Switzerland, but Skype and time-zone differences frustrated us. His 2008 book – *A Happy Customer Tells Three People, an Unhappy Customer Tells 3,000* – was a great resource, as was his wisdom as a colleague on the P&G board.

I met Dave Carroll three years ago at a conference organized by the Society for New Communications Research. Although I didn't interview him for this book, his appropriately titled *United Breaks Guitars* book came out while we were finalizing this one. It's a great read and a fascinating tale of nearly overnight success driven by word of mouth.

Another book that influenced me greatly was *A Complaint is a Gift*. If you need to explain to your management why embracing critics is a good idea, then that book has all the ammunition you need. Jane Jordan-Meier sent me a copy of her *Four Stages of Highly Effective Crisis Management* as a thank-you for an interview I did with her back in 2009 and I liked it so much that it became the framework for Chapter 10. Other helpful books included Guy Kawasaki's *Enchantment* and Katie Paine's *Measure What Matters*.

Michelle Davidson is a great copyeditor. Lori Faure searched far and wide for the perfect cover photo and matched it with a terrific design.

Finally, this book and the four that preceded it over the past five years wouldn't have been possible without the unceasing love and support of my wife (and primary editor), Dana. Not only does she help sharpen my prose and fix my mistakes, but she has always encouraged me to satisfy my innate curiosity. Eight months after the birth of our twin daughters, I announced that I wanted to start this book. She sighed, smiled and said, "Go get 'em, babe."

— Paul Gillin

Index

About the Authors

Dana Gillin photo

Paul Gillin is a writer, speaker and online marketing consultant who specializes in helping businesses use content to reach customers. A popular speaker and writer, he has addressed more than 100 groups and published more than 150 articles since 2008. He is a veteran technology journalist with more than 25 years of editorial experience, including 13 years exclusively online.

His books include *The New Influencers*, *Secrets of Social Media Marketing*, *The Joy of Geocaching* (co-authored with wife Dana) and *Social Marketing to the Business Customer* (co-authored with Eric Schwartzman). Paul is a columnist for *BtoB* magazine and a director of the Society for New Communications Research. His blogs are PaulGillin.com and NewspaperDeathWatch.com.

Greg Gianforte has started five successful software companies. He founded RightNow Technologies in 1997 with a mission to rid the world of bad experiences. The company enjoyed 15 years of continuous growth. At the time of its sale to Oracle in 2011, it had more than 2,000 large customers, 1,100 employees and $225 million in annual revenue.

Among his many awards are Ernst & Young's Pacific Northwest Entrepreneur of the Year and the Leader Award from *CRM* magazine. he was inducted into the CRM Hall of Fame in 2007.

His books include *Bootstrapping Your Business* and *Eight to Great: Eight Steps to Delivering an Exceptional Customer Experience*.

Footnotes

Introduction

[1] Owyang, Jeremiah, Andrew Jones, Christine Tran, and Andrew Nguyen, "Social Business Readiness: How Advanced Companies Prepare Internally," Altimeter Group. Last modified August 31, 2011.

Chapter 1: When Customers Attack

[1] The page is still live at http://www.facebook.com/groups/230956705705 (accessed August 15, 2012).

[2] Byron, Ellen, "P&G Goes on Offensive for Pampers," *The Wall Street Journal*, June 14, 2010, http://online.wsj.com/article/SB10001424052748703685404575306863979636250.html (accessed August 15, 2012).

[3] "No Specific Cause Found Yet Linking Dry Max Diapers to Diaper Rash," CPSC press release, September 2, 2010.

[4] "Are Twitter and Facebook changing the way we complain?" BBC News, May 12, 2012, http://www.bbc.co.uk/news/uk-18081651 (accessed July 8, 2012).

[5] Shandwick, Weber and Spencer Stuart, "The Rising CCO IV," June 2012, http://www.webershandwick.com/resources/ws/Rising_CCO_IV.pdf (accessed July 8, 2012).

[6] Burson-Marsteller and Penn Schoen Berland, "Crisis Preparedness Survey," May 2012, http://burson-marsteller.eu/wp-

content/uploads/2012/06/BM_Crisis-Brochure_14-06_prod.pdf (accessed July 8, 2012).

[7] Webber, Allan, Charlene Li and Jaimy Szymanski, "Guarding the Social Gates: The Imperative for Social Media Risk Management," Altimeter Group, http://www.slideshare.net/Altimeter/guarding-the-social-gates-the-imperative-for-social-media-risk-management (accessed August 15, 2012). Last modified August 8, 2012.

[8] "Customer Experience Report, North America, 2010," RightNow Technologies, http://www.rightnow.com/files/analyst-reports/RightNow-Customer-Experience-Impact-North-America-Report.pdf.

[9] 2012 Brand Loyalty Survey, ClickFox, March 2012, http://web.clickfox.com/2012SurveyResults-BrandLoyalty.html.

[10] Bell, Simon J. and James A. Luddington, "Coping With Customer Complaints," *Journal of Service Research* 8, February 2006, pp. 221-233.

[11] Zetlin, Minda, "Listening to Complainers Is Bad for Your Brain." Inc., August 20, 2012, http://www.inc.com/minda-zetlin/listening-to-complainers-is-bad-for-your-brain.html (accessed August 21, 2012).

Chapter 2: How Attacks Happen

[1] Knowles, David, "Partners In 'Slime," *The Daily*, March 5, 2012, http://www.thedaily.com/page/2012/03/05/030512-news-pink-slime-1-3 (accessed July 28, 2012).

[2] Siegel, Bettina, "Tell USDA to STOP Using Pink Slime in School Food!" Change.org, http://www.Change.org/petitions/tell-usda-to-stop-using-pink-slime-in-school-food (accessed July 28, 2012). Last modified March 30, 2012.

[3] *Food Safety News* has an excellent timeline of the pink slime crisis at http://www.foodsafetynews.com/2012/04/bpi-and-pink-slime-a-timeline/.

[4] Fielding, Michael, Dani Friedland, Rita Jane Gabbett, Tom Johnston and Lisa M. Keefe, "Slimed: What the Hell Happened," *Meatingplace*, May 2012, p. 20.

[5] "Report Roundup: Demographics," eMarketer, March 21, 2011. http://www.emarketer.com/blog/index.php/report-roundup-demographics/

[6] "Crashing Motrin-Gate: A Social-Media Case Study," Advertising Age, November 24, 2008, http://adage.com/article/news/crashing-motrin-gate-a-social-media-case-study/132787 (accessed July 28, 2012).

[7] The first tweet about the ad was posted at 10:28 p.m. by Amy Gates of the CrunchyDomesticGoddess blog, according to Advertising Age. Gottlieb's tweet, which appeared a half hour later, was the first to use the #MotrinMoms hash tag.

[8] Presnal, Katja, "Motrin Ad Makes Moms Mad," YouTube, posted November 16, 2008, http://www.youtube.com/watch?v=LhR-y1N6R8Q&feature=youtu.be.

[9] Shankman, Peter, "The Real Problem with the Motrin Ads...." Peter Shankman (blog), November 16, 2008, http://shankman.com/the-real-problem-with-the-motrin-ads (accessed August 15, 2012).

[10] Sierra, Christine, "Should Motrin have Pulled its Babywearing Ad? #Motrinmoms By the Numbers," Lexablog, November 20, 2008, http://www.lexalytics.com/lexablog/2008/should-motrin-have-pulled-its-babywearing-ad-motrinmoms-numbers (accessed August 15, 2012).

[11] Paine, Katie Delahaye, *Measure What Matters* (Hoboken, NJ: John Wiley & Sons, 2011), p. 179.

[12] Barlow, Janelle and Claus Møller, *A Complaint is a Gift* (San Francisco: Berrett-Koehler Publishers, 1996), p. 159.

[13] Miller, Kivi Leroux, "The Accidental Rebranding of Komen for the Cure," Nonprofit Marketing Guide (blog), February 1, 2012, http://www.nonprofitmarketingguide.com/blog/2012/02/01/the-accidental-rebranding-of-komen-for-the-cure (accessed July 28, 2012).

[14] York, Dan, "Watching The Colossal PR Train Wreck Of The Susan G. Komen / Planned Parenthood Debacle," Disruptive Conversations (blog), February 2, 2012, http://www.disruptiveconversations.com/2012/02/watching-the-colossal-pr-train-wreck-of-the-susan-g-komen-planned-parenthood-debacle.html (accessed July 28, 2012).

[15] Hobson, Neville and Shel Holtz, "The Hobson & Holtz Report - Podcast #637," For Immediate Release (podcast), February 6, 2012, http://www.forimmediaterelease.biz/index.php?/weblog/comments/the _hobson_holtz_report_-_podcast_637_february_6_2012 (accessed July 28, 2012).

[16] Handel made lemonade from lemons. In August, she announced she was writing a book about the affair entitled "Planned Bullyhood."

[17] Hensley, Scott, "Planned Parenthood Controversy Hangs Over Komen's Fundraising Races," NPR Health Blog, June 1, 2012, http://www.npr.org/blogs/health/2012/06/01/154135526/planned-parenthood-controversy-hangs-over-komens-fundraising-races (accessed July 28, 2012).

[18] Divol, Roxanne, David Edelman and Hugo Sarrazin, "Demystifying social media," *McKinsey Quarterly*, April 2012, https://www.mckinseyquarterly.com/Demystifying_social_media_2958 (accessed July 28, 2012).

Chapter 3: Studies in Social Media Crisis

[1] The blog entry containing the embedded SlideShare presentation can be found at http://www.karlhavard.com/2009/07/aviva-worst-customer-service-possible.html.

[2] A more detailed description of this case with many more accompanying metrics can be found in Somatica's "Online Reputation Management Via the Social Web," posted August 13, 2009, http://www.slideshare.net/Somatica/somatica-digital-reputation-management-case-study-on-aviva-310809.

[3] This story is documented in more detail in Ron Ploof's excellent e-book, "The Ranger Station Fire: How Ford Motor Company Used Social Media to Extinguish a PR Fire in Less Than 24 Hours," which can be downloaded from Ploof's blog at http://ronamok.com/ebooks/the_ranger_station_fire_final.pdf.

[4] Li, Charlene, *Open Leadership: How Social Technology Can Transform the Way You Lead* (Hoboken, NJ: John Wiley & Sons, 2010).

[5] "Walgreens Enlists Paid Social-Media Warriors in Battle With Express Scripts," *Advertising Age*, January 12, 2012,

http://adage.com/article/news/walgreens-turns-paid-bloggers-express-scripts-battle/232082/.

[6] Biggs, John, "A Dispute Over Who Owns a Twitter Account Goes to Court." *The New York Times*, December 25, 2011, http://www.nytimes.com/2011/12/26/technology/lawsuit-may-determine-who-owns-a-twitter-account.html?_r=1 (accessed July 8, 2012).

[7] Holm, Erik, "We're Not MF Global!! Clarifies FM Global," *The Wall Street Journal*, December 8, 2011, http://blogs.wsj.com/deals/2011/12/08/were-not-mf-global-clarifies-fm-global (accessed July 8, 2012).

[8] Primack, Dan, "FM Global is not the same as MF Global," CNN Money (blog), December 8, 2011, http://finance.fortune.cnn.com/2011/12/08/fm-global-is-not-the-same-as-mf-global (accessed July 8, 2012).

[9] Fisher, Matt, "My Sister Paid Progressive Insurance to Defend Her Killer In Court," Premium Fisher (blog), August 13, 2012, http://mattfisher.tumblr.com/post/29338478278/my-sister-paid-progressive-insurance-to-defend-her (accessed August 31, 2012).

[10] A repost is similar to a re-tweet. Tumblr users can copy a fragment of another Tumblr post to their own blogs with two clicks. This simple amplification method can grow awareness very quickly.

[11] Progressive Insurance, "Update on the Kaitlynn Fisher Case," Understanding Insurance (blog), August 16, 2012, http://www.progressive.com/understanding-insurance/entries/2012/8/16/update_on_the_kaitl.aspx (accessed August 31, 2012).

[12] Roberts, Hannah, "#McFail! McDonalds' Twitter promotion backfires as users hijack #McDstories hash tag to share fast food horror stories," *The Daily Mail*, January 24, 2012, http://www.dailymail.co.uk/news/article-2090862/McDstories-McDonalds-Twitter-promotion-backfires-users-share-fast-food-horror-stories.html (accessed July 11, 2012).

Chapter 4: Why Customers Attack

[1] FieldsDayProds, "Bob Garfield on Nightline," YouTube, March 26, 2008, http://youtu.be/1a2R8wKfmHM.

[2] Winch, Guy, "Why We Get Angry About Customer Service." *Psychology Today*, June 6, 2012, http://www.psychologytoday.com/blog/the-squeaky-wheel/201206/why-we-get-angry-about-customer-service (accessed July 25, 2012).

[3] Friele, Roland D. and Emmy M. Sluijs, "Patient expectations of fair complaint handling in hospitals: empirical data." BMC Health Services Research, 2006, p. 106, http://www.ncbi.nlm.nih.gov/pmc/articles/PMC1560118/pdf/1472-6963-6-106.pdf (accessed August 17, 2012).

[4] Bitner, Mary Jo, Bernard H. Booms and Lois A. Mohr, "Critical Service Encounters: The Employee's Viewpoint," *Journal of Marketing*, 58, October 1994, pp. 95-106.

[5] Barlow, Janelle and Claus Møller, *A Complaint is a Gift*, (San Francisco: Berrett-Koehler, 1996), p. 125.

[6] Holmes, David, "World's Coolest Flight Attendant," YouTube, http://www.youtube.com/watch?v=-_MfHMQWmiE.

[7] Nuts About Southwest, "The GAAP RAP by Southwest Airlines Rapping Flight Attendant," YouTube, May 20, 2009, http://www.youtube.com/watch?v=7P2-vEtXSug.

[8] Owyang, Jeremiah, Andrew Jones, Christine Tran and Andrew Nguyen, "Social Business Readiness: How Advanced Companies Prepare Internally," Altimeter Group Research Report, August 11, 2011, http://www.slideshare.net/jeremiah_owyang/social-readiness-how-advanced-companies-prepare (accessed July 25, 2012).

[9] We're grateful to Altimeter Group's Jeremiah Owyang for sharing with us the raw data used in preparing the Social Business Readiness report for our analysis.

[10] Pulsepoint Group and *The Economist* Intelligence Unit, "The Economics of the Socially Engaged Enterprise," March 2012,

http://www.pulsepointgroup.com/staging.pulsepoint/wp-content/uploads/2012/03/AP-Presentation-3_22_12-final.pdf.

[11] "Ryanair deny that heart attack passenger charged for sandwich," Independent.ie, August 5, 2011, http://www.independent.ie/todays-paper/ryanair-deny-that-heart-attack-passenger-charged-for-sandwich-2841266.html (accessed July 25, 2012).

[12] "Passengers attack Spirit Airlines for new carry-on fees," New York *Daily News*, August 2, 2010, http://www.nydailynews.com/news/money/passengers-attack-spirit-airlines-carry-on-fees-article-1.200209#ixzz1wZeqRmBS (accessed July 25, 2012).

Chapter 5: The Attackers

[1] "United Breaks Guitars" was actually a trilogy of three songs, but the first one got all the attention: Sons of Maxwell, "United Breaks Guitars," YouTube, posted July 6, 2009, http://www.youtube.com/watch?v=5YGc4zOqozo.

[2] One of many online copies can be found at http://www.slideshare.net/politicsjunkie/yours-is-a-very-bad-hotel. The hotel today is a Four Points by Sheraton.

[3] Bly, Laura, "Online complaint about hotel service scores," *USA Today*, January 4, 2002, http://www.usatoday.com/tech/news/2002/01/04/online-hotel-complaint.htm (accessed July 8, 2012).

[4] Hosenkamp, Samantha, "McDonald's media relations chief explains the best and worst things to do in a crisis," Ragan's PR Daily, December 6, 2011, http://www.prdaily.com/Main/Articles/10215.aspx (accessed July 19, 2012).

[5] "Hoteliers accuse Tripadvisor reviewers of blackmail," *The Week*, November 22, 2011, http://www.theweek.co.uk/uk-news/42894/hoteliers-accuse-tripadvisor-reviewers-blackmail (accessed July 11, 2012).

[6] Pfeifer, Stuart and E. Scott Reckard, "One Facebook post becomes national movement to abandon big banks," *The Los Angeles Times*, November 4, 2011, http://articles.latimes.com/2011/nov/04/business/la-fi-bank-transfer-20111105 (accessed July 11, 2012).

[7] "The 2012 TIME 100 Poll," March 29, 2012, http://www.time.com/time/specials/packages/article/0,28804,2107952_2107953_2109996,00.html (accessed July 21, 2012). At last report, both Christian and Katchpole had launched new careers as campaign organizers and consumer activism consultants.

[8] McCarthy, Caroline, "Nestle mess shows sticky side of Facebook pages," CNet, March 19, 2010, http://news.cnet.com/8301-13577_3-20000805-36.html (accessed July 21, 2012).

[9] Rose, Frank, "Commercial Break," *Wired*, December 2006, http://www.wired.com/wired/archive/14.12/tahoe_pr.html (accessed July 13, 2012).

[10] Barlow and Møller, Complaint, pp. 107-113.

[11] White, Nicole, "TSA Agents Took My Son," My Bottle's Up (blog), October 16, 2009, http://www.mybottlesup.com/2009/10/tsa-agents-took-my-son (accessed July 14, 2012).

[12] Blogger Bob, "Response to 'TSA Agents Took My Son'," The TSA Blog (blog), October 16, 2009, http://blog.tsa.gov/2009/10/response-to-tsa-agents-took-my-son.html (accessed July 14, 2012).

Chapter 6: Ordnance

[1] Jeff Jarvis, who instigated "Dell Hell" in 2005, recapped the story two years later in "Dell Hell: The end?" October 18, 2007, http://buzzmachine.com/2007/10/18/dell-hell-the-end/ (accessed July 21, 2012).

[2] This story is told on Google Blogosoped: "Vincent Ferrari, One of the New Influencers," June 4, 2007, http://blogoscoped.com/archive/2007-06-04-n80.html (accessed July 21, 2012).

[3] Barnes, Nora Ganim and Ava M. Lescault, "The 2012 *Inc.* 500 Social Media Update: Blogging Declines As Newer Tools Rule," University of Massachusetts at Dartmouth, http://www.umassd.edu/cmr/studiesandresearch/2012inc500socialmedia update (accessed July 21, 2012).

[4] "State of the Blogosphere 2011," Technorati, November 4, 2011, http://technorati.com/social-media/article/state-of-the-blogosphere-2011-part1 (accessed July 21, 2012).

[5] Gillin, Paul, "General Mills' Blogger Relations Program Follows the Golden Rule," paulgillin.com (blog), July 29, 2010, http://support.awarenessnetworks.com/Main/content/?id=69206198759 95272388&type=post&uid=9130202349092311122 (accessed July 21, 2012).

[6] Martin, Tracy and Sybrina Fulton, "Prosecute the killer of our son, 17-year-old Trayvon Martin," Change.org, April 11, 2012, http://www.Change.org/petitions/prosecute-the-killer-of-our-son-17-year-old-trayvon-martin, (accessed July 21, 2012).

[7] Alter, Jonathan, "For Change.org, a Better World Is Clicks Away," Bloomberg View, March 8, 2012, http://www.bloomberg.com/news/2012-03-09/for-change-org-better-world-is-clicks-away-commentary-by-jonathan-alter.html (accessed July 21, 2012).

[8] Rip-off Report's quirky founder, Ed Magedson, appears to revel in controversy. He cheerfully tells inquiring reporters how many times he's been sued while also pointing out that no action has yet been successful. His policy of not removing critical reviews has drawn considerable fire, but Magedson stands behind it. A page on the site titled "About Us: Want to sue Ripoff Report?" runs to more than 8,000 words and includes an analysis of the Communications Decency Act, among other things. A 2007 feature article in the *Phoenix New Times* has considerably more detail at http://www.phoenixnewtimes.com/2007-02-01/news/the-real-rip-off-report (accessed July 21, 2012).

[9] Nudd, Tim, "ChapStick Gets Itself in a Social Media Death Spiral," *Adweek*, October 26, 2011, http://www.adweek.com/adfreak/chapstick-gets-itself-social-media-death-spiral-136097 (accessed July 18, 2012).

[10] The terms are visible at http://www.facebook.com/legal/terms

[11] http://www.facebook.com/BPAmerica/app_6009294086

[12] Segal, David, "The Dirty Little Secrets of Search," *The New York Times*, February 12, 2011, http://www.nytimes.com/2011/02/13/business/13search.html (accessed July 15, 2012).

[13] Moran explored negative SEO in more detail on his blog in "What Google Could Do to Stop Negative SEO," http://www.biznology.com/2008/03/what_google_could_do_to_stop_n

[14] Warzel, Charlie, "BuzzFeed Report to Publishing Partners Demonstrates Power of Social Web Reddit generates huge referral traffic while Pinterest falls flat," *Adweek*, August 29, 2012, http://www.adweek.com/news/technology/buzzfeed-report-publishing-partners-demonstrates-power-social-web-143194 (accessed September 6, 2012).

[15] Wikipedia contributors, "Reddit," Wikipedia, The Free Encyclopedia, http://en.wikipedia.org/w/index.php?title=Reddit&oldid=510945758 (accessed September 6, 2012).

[16] "ShareThis and Starcom MediaVest Group Collaborate to Release First Comprehensive Study on Sharing," ShareThis press release, June 6, 2011, http://blog.sharethis.com/2011/06/06/sharethis-and-starcom-mediavest-group-collaborate-to-release-first-comprehensive-study-on-sharing (accessed July 18, 2012).

[17] *Occupying Wall Street: The Inside Story of an Action that Changed America* (New York and London: OR Books, 2011) p. 156.

[18] Cheng, Alex and Mark Evans, "An In-Depth Look Inside the Twitter World," Sysomos Resource Library, June 2009, http://www.sysomos.com/insidetwitter (accessed July 21, 2012).

[19] The author turned out to be Josh Simpson, a 26-year-old aspiring comedian from Los Angeles whose career has no doubt been boosted at BP's expense.

[20] There are scores of these tools on the market but few comprehensive ratings guides. Two places to look are Bulldog Reporter's PR Monitoring & Measurement Software Buyer's Guide (http://www.bulldogreporter.com/2012-pr-monitoring-buyers-buyers-guide-comparison-chart) and the Social Media Monitoring Category of TopTen Reviews (http://social-media-monitoring-review.toptenreviews.com/). Be careful when relying on Google search for evaluations because the market changes rapidly and many top Google results are three or more years old.

[21] "Holy Nyans! 60 hours per minute and 4 billion views a day on YouTube," The Official YouTube Blog, January 23, 2012,

http://youtube-global.blogspot.com/2012/01/holy-nyans-60-hours-per-minute-and-4.html (accessed July 21, 2012).

[22] Neff, Jack, "Dove Viral Draws Heat From Critics," *Advertising Age*, November 26, 2007, http://adage.com/article/news/dove-viral-draws-heat-critics/122185 (accessed July 21, 2012).

[23] Barnes and Lescault, "The 2012 *Inc.* 500 Social Media Update."

[24] "Terms of Service," GM Fast Lane Blog, http://fastlane.gmblogs.com/?page_id=1486 (accessed July 21, 2012).

[25] "User Agreement," Delta blog, http://blog.delta.com/user-agreement (accessed July 21, 2012).

[26] "Evolution (advertisement)," Wikipedia, http://en.wikipedia.org/wiki/Evolution_(advertisement) (accessed July 21, 2012).

[27] Philips, Wilson, "Chow Down (at Chick-fil-A)," http://www.youtube.com/watch?v=sO-msplukrw (accessed July 21, 2012).

[28] "'Chow Down (At Chick-Fil-A),' Wilson Phillips Drag Spoof, Parodies Fast Food Chain's 'Anti-Gay' Controversy." The Huffington Post, March 19, 2012, http://www.huffingtonpost.com/2012/03/19/chow-down-at-chick-fil-a-wilson-phillips-drag-spoof_n_1365170.html (accessed July 21, 2012).

[1] "TripAdvisor," Wikipedia, http://en.wikipedia.org/wiki/Tripadvisor#cite_note-18 (accessed July 22, 2012).

[2] "10 Things You Should Know about Yelp," Yelp.com, http://www.yelp.com/about (accessed July 22, 2012).

[3] Ghose, A. and P.G. Ipeirotis, "Estimating the Helpfulness and Economic Impact of Product Reviews: Mining Text and Reviewer Characteristics," *IEEE Transactions on Knowledge and Data Engineering*, 23, no. 10 (2011), pp. 1498-1512, http://pages.stern.nyu.edu/~panos/publications/tkde2010-usefulness.pdf (accessed August 18, 2012). This is just one example of academic research that has gone into understanding customer reviews. The New York University professors examined the effect of factors such as subjectivity, readability and even spelling mistakes on the perceived

helpfulness of reviews and correlated those factors with product sales. Their reference list points to many other resources about how customer reviews affect buying behavior.

4 Hosford, Christopher, "Fraudulent social reviews, both positive and negative, on the rise," *BtoB*, October 10, 2012, http://www.btobonline.com/article/20121010/STRATEGY02/3101099 99/fraudulent-social-reviews-both-positive-and-negative-on-the-rise (accessed October 11, 2012).

5 Streitfeld, David, "The Best Book Reviews Money Can Buy," *The New York Times*, August 25, 2012, http://www.nytimes.com/2012/08/26/business/book-reviewers-for-hire-meet-a-demand-for-online-raves.html (accessed October 11, 2012).

6 Charman-Anderson, Suw, "Fake Reviews: Amazon's Rotten Core," *Forbes*, August 28, 2012, http://www.forbes.com/sites/suwcharmananderson/2012/08/28/fake-reviews-amazons-rotten-core (accessed October 11, 2012).

7 Moyer, Michael, "Manipulation of the Crowd: How Trustworthy Are Online Ratings?" *Scientific American*, July 2010, http://www.scientificamerican.com/article.cfm?id=manipulation-of-the-crowd (accessed July 23, 2012).

8 Barone, Lisa, "How Companies Should Respond To Negative Reviews," Outspoken Media (blog), April 13, 2009. http://outspokenmedia.com/reputation-management/respond-negative-reviews.

9 "Customer Satisfaction Surveys: Opening the Door to Customer Engagement," Chadwick Martin Bailey Consumer Pulse, Feb., 2012. http://www.cmbinfo.com/cmb-cms/wp-content/uploads/2012/02/Consumer-Pulse_CSS_final_2012.pdf (accessed July 25, 2012).

10 Luca, Michael, "Reviews, Reputation, and Revenue: The Case of Yelp.com," Working Paper, September 16, 2011, http://www.hbs.edu/research/pdf/12-016.pdf (accessed July 25, 2012).

11 "Review users show 98% higher revenue per visitor for Epson," Bazaarvoice case study, November 11, 2010, http://www.bazaarvoice.com/resources/case-studies/review-users-show-98-higher-revenue-visitor-epson (accessed July 25, 2012).

[12] Alsever, Jennifer, "Even bad reviews boost sales," CNN Money, September 28, 2009,
http://money.cnn.com/2009/09/28/smallbusiness/retail_democracy.fsb
/index.htm (accessed July 25, 2012).

[13] "2012 Brand Loyalty Survey," ClickFox, April 2012,
http://web.clickfox.com/rs/clickfox/images/cf-survey-results-brand-loyalty.pdf (accessed July 25, 2012).

[14] Nelson, E., "Why Terrible Online Reviews Are Actually Good For You," AdAge Digital, September 15, 2011,
http://adage.com/article/digitalnext/terrible-online-reviews-good/229790 (accessed May 25, 2012).

[15] "Teleflora Drives Sales with a Bouquet of Social Offerings," PowerReviews.com case study, 2012,
http://www.powerreviews.com/resources/casestudies/teleflora-drives-sales-bouquet-social-offerings (accessed August 19, 2012).

[16] Barrera, Alex, "The natural ubiquity of the J-curve," Bazaarvoice: blog, December 21, 2011,
http://www.bazaarvoice.com/blog/2011/12/21/the-natural-ubiquity-of-the-j-curve (accessed August 19, 2012).

[17] Berger, J., "Bad Reviews Can Boost Sales. Here's Why," *Harvard Business Review*, March 2012, http://hbr.org/2012/03/bad-reviews-can-boost-sales-heres-why/ar/1 (accessed July 25, 2012).

Chapter 8: Mainstream Media — Enabler or Enforcer?

[1] Appelbaum, Binyamin, "Joe Weisenthal vs. the 24-Hour News Cycle." *The New York Times*, May 10, 2012,
http://www.nytimes.com/2012/05/13/magazine/joe-weisenthal-vs-the-24-hour-news-cycle.html (accessed August 27, 2012).

[2] The Huffington Post, "OffTheBus Submission Guidelines,"
http://www.huffingtonpost.com/p/offthebus-submission-guid.html (accessed August 27, 2012).

[3] Schonfeld, Erick, "Six Months In, And 600 Posts Later . . . The Worlds Of Blogging and Journalism Collide (In My Brain)," TechCrunch.com

(blog), March 30, 2008, http://techcrunch.com/2008/03/30/six-months-in-and-600-posts-later-the-worlds-of-blogging-and-journalism-collide-in-my-brain (accessed October 8, 2012).

⁴ Gillin, Paul, "How New Influencers are Reinventing Journalism," paulgillin.com (blog), April 17, 2008, http://gillin.com/blog/2008/04/how-new-influencers-are-reinventing-journalism. It should be noted that since its acquisition by *Consumer Reports*, The Consumerist has adopted a more rigorous approach to fact-checking.

5 Clifford, Stephanie, "Survey Finds Slack Editing on Magazine Web Sites," *The New York Times*, February 8, 2010, http://ow.ly/ejsuW.

6 The Folger Library in Washington, D.C., presented some examples of these crude early attempts at journalism in a 2008 exhibit summarized at http://newspaperdeathwatch.com/a-distant-mirror.

7 Wikipedia has some vivid examples of how hyperbole trumped fact in the days of yellow journalism at http://en.wikipedia.org/wiki/Yellow_journalism.

8 Wikipedia has a thorough account of the many studies that have measured its accuracy at http://en.wikipedia.org/wiki/Wikipedia_accuracy.

9 Lacy, Sarah, "Who the Hell Is Enrolling in Journalism School Right Now?" TechCrunch (blog), April 8, 2009, http://techcrunch.com/2009/04/08/who-the-hell-is-enrolling-in-journalism-school-right-now (accessed July 27, 2012).

10 Craig Silverman documents media screw-ups on his deadpan RegretTheError.com website. Needless to say, he's not hurting for material these days.

11 Brienza, Victoria, "The 10 Worst Jobs of 2012," CareerCast.com, April 2012, http://www.careercast.com/jobs-rated/10-worst-jobs-2012 (accessed July 28, 2012).

12 "3rd Annual Survey of the Media in the Wired World," Society of New Communications Research and Middleberg Communications, May 2011, http://www.slideshare.net/sncr/how-are-media-journalism-evolving.

13 Warner, Andrew, "How Can You Manipulate The Media To Promote Your Self-Interest? – with Ryan Holiday," Mixergy.com, July 20, 2012, http://mixergy.com/ryan-holiday-interview (accessed July 28, 2012).

[14] Paine, Katie Delahaye, *Measure What Matters* (Hoboken, NJ: John Wiley & Sons, 2011), p. 169.

Chapter 9: An Ounce of Prevention

[1] There are more than 250 free and paid social media monitoring services, by some estimates. Comparative reports can run to several thousand dollars, but Bulldog Reporter's 2012 PR Measurement and Monitoring Software Buyer's Guide is a good free starting point: http://www.bulldogreporter.com/daily-dog/2012-pr-monitoring-buyers-guide.

[2] This is completely self-serving, but Dell Tech Center is covered in the first chapter of *Social Marketing to the Business Customer* by Paul Gillin and Eric Schwartzman (Hoboken, N.J.: John Wiley & Sons, 2011).

[3] Fishburn-Hedges, "18 million customers flooding social networks to speak to brands," May 2012, http://www.fishburn-hedges.co.uk/news/articles/18-million-customers-flooding-social-networks-speak-brands (accessed November 8, 2012).

[4] Social Media Today, "The Social Customer Service Conflict," (infographic), October, 2012, http://2012.pivotcon.com/wp-content/uploads/2012/10/SAPInfographic_FINAL-02.jpg (accessed October 17, 2012).

[5] eMarketer, "Are Brands Ignoring Facebook's Interactive Potential?" March 1, 2012, http://www.emarketer.com/Article.aspx?id=1008873&R=1008873 (accessed November 8, 2012).

[6] "Are Twitter and Facebook changing the way we complain?" BBC, May 17, 2012, http://www.bbc.co.uk/news/uk-18081651 (accessed November 8, 2012).

[7] American Express, "Social Media Raises the Stakes for Customer Service," May 2, 2012, http://about.americanexpress.com/news/pr/2012/gcsb.aspx (accessed November 8, 2012).

[8] Baer, Jay, "Are Consumer Expectations For Social Customer Service Realistic?," The Social Habit (blog), October, 2012,

http://socialhabit.com/uncategorized/customer-service-expectations (accessed October 18, 2012)

9 Divol, Roxane, David Edelman and Hugo Sarrazin, "Demystifying social media," *McKinsey Quarterly*, April 2012, http://www.mckinseyquarterly.com/Demystifying_social_media_2958 (accessed November 8, 2012).

10 Knowledge@Wharton, "Want to Improve Customer Service? Treat Your Employees Better," March 14, 2012, http://knowledge.wharton.upenn.edu/article.cfm?articleid=2954 (accessed November 8, 2012).

11 "Influencer" isn't really a word, as Microsoft Office never tires of telling us. The correct word is "influential," but people seem to like "influencer" better. We hope Microsoft eventually comes around.

12 Paul likes Klout as much as he likes cauliflower, which is not at all. It's not so much because of what Klout does as for what it claims to be: "The Standard of Influence." His primal scream therapy is at "The Trouble with Klout." paulgillin.com (blog), September 6, 2011, http://gillin.com/blog/2011/09/the-trouble-with-klout.

13 Solis, Brian, "The Rise of Digital Influence," Altimeter Group, 2012, p. 7, http://www.slideshare.net/Altimeter/the-rise-of-digital-influence (accessed July 11, 2012).

14 Hayes, Nick and Duncan Brown,"Are Your Customers Influenced Online, Offline or Both?" Influencer50 white paper, November 28, 2011, http://influencermarketingreview.com/2011/11/28/new-white-paper-from-influencer50-are-your-customers-influenced-online-offline-or-both (accessed August 8, 2012).

15 At the risk of belaboring the point, even broad measures of influence may fail to take into account gender, age and other situational factors. Researchers Sinan Aral and Dylan Walker of New York University studied the spread of a Facebook app to measure influence and found, among other things:

- Men are more influential than women;

- Women influence men more than they influence other women;

- People over 30 are more influential and less susceptible to influence than younger people;

- Married people are the least susceptible to the influence of others in the decision to purchase a product;

- Influential people tend to be less susceptible to the influence of others, and people who are susceptible to influence tended not to be influential themselves.

In short, influence measurement resists oversimplification, which is another reason Klout is cauliflower. See Aral, Sinan and Dylan Walker, "Identifying Influential and Susceptible Members of Social Networks," *Science*, 1215842. Published online June 21, 2012 (DOI:10.1126/science.1215842).

[16] Don't believe us? As of this writing, a site called Intertwitter.com was offering to sell 100,000 Twitter followers for just $487. Facebook has acknowledged that nearly 9% of its accounts are fake, and a U.K. company called Status People created a tool to identify likely fake followers for any Twitter account (http://fakers.statuspeople.com/Fakers).

[17] Eloqua, submission to the Society for New Communications Research Excellence in New Media Communications Awards, 2010, http://sncr.org/node/114.

Chapter 10: Handling an Attack

[1] Gerber, Lisa, "How to Decrease Response Time on Negative Comments," Social Media Sun, June 2012, http://socialmediasun.com/decrease-response-time-on-negative-comments (accessed August 10, 2012).

[2] If you don't think Pinterest is a potential problem for you, consider what could happen if photos of your product bursting into flame or of your delivery man smoking a joint began being re-pinned en masse.

[3] "The WOMMA Guide to Disclosure in Social Media Marketing," http://womma.org/ethics/disclosure/. Last modified August 2012.

[4] You can read a good case study of PepsiCo's employee social media training program at http://sncr.org/node/445.

[5] We increasingly hear of companies demanding access to the Facebook accounts of employees or job applicants. We think this is an invasion of privacy because much of what happens on Facebook goes on between

small circles of select friends. The courts haven't ruled on the legality of this tactic, but even if it turns out to be legal, it's a lousy way to build trust with your people.

[6] Jordan-Meier, Jane, *The Four Stages of Highly Effective Crisis Management: How to Manage the Media in the Digital Age* (Boca Raton, FL: CRC Press, 2011) p. 50.

[7] Progressive Insurance, "Update on the Kaitlynn Fisher Case," Understanding Insurance (blog), August 16, 2012, http://www.progressive.com/understanding-insurance/entries/2012/8/16/update_on_the_kaitl.aspx (accessed August 27, 2012).

[8] Progresso used this statement in defending its use of bisphenol A (BPA) in its soup cans. http://bit.ly/ProgressoBPA.

[9] Hobson, Neville, "FIR Speakers and Speeches: Neville Hobson on Reputation Management at Internet Speed," For Immediate Release (podcast), May 16, 2012, http://www.forimmediaterelease.biz/index.php?/weblog/comments/fir_speakers_and_speeches_neville_hobson_on_reputation_management/ (accessed August 27, 2012).

[10] Sayare, Scott, "For Results, Twitter Gets Out Early Word, in Code," *The New York Times*, April 22, 2012, http://www.nytimes.com/2012/04/23/world/europe/french-use-twitter-to-share-early-election-results.html (accessed August 27, 2012).

[11] "FedEx Response to Customer Video," YouTube, uploaded December 21, 2011, http://www.youtube.com/watch?v=4ESU_PcqI38.

[12] CIPR Social Media Guidelines (updated January 2009), http://www.cipr.co.uk/sites/default/files/Social%20Media%20Guidelines.pdf

[13] http://en.wikipedia.org/wiki/Astroturfing

Chapter 11: The Attack-Resistant Organization

[1] Peppers, Don and Martha Rogers, *Extreme Trust* (New York: Portfolio/Penguin), p. 1.

[2] "The New Realities of 'Dating' in the Digital Age," Accenture 2011 Global Consumer Research Study, http://www.accenture.com/SiteCollectionDocuments/PDF/Accenture-Global-Consumer-Research-New-Realities.pdf (accessed August 7, 2012).

[3] "2012 Brand Loyalty Survey," ClickFox, April 2012, http://web.clickfox.com/2012SurveyResults-BrandLoyalty.html (accessed August 7, 2012).

[4] "Report: The Future of Customer Experience," Temkin Group, August 6, 2012, http://experiencematters.wordpress.com/2012/08/06/report-the-future-of-customer-experience/ (accessed Aug. 14, 2012).

[5] American Customer Satisfaction Index, "National Quarterly Scores," continuously updated, http://www.theacsi.org/acsi-results/national-quarterly-scores (accessed October 18, 2012).

[6] CDC Software, "Research Reveals Customer Service Satisfaction is at an All-time Low as Retailers and Leisure Companies Prepare for Vital Pre-Christmas Sales Period" (press release), September 15, 2011, http://www.cdcsoftware.com/en/About-Us/News-and-Events/Press-Releases/2011/20110915-Research-Reveals-Customer-Service-Satisfaction-is-at-an-All-time-Low-as (accessed October 18, 2012).

[7] "Customer Experience Report, North America, 2011," RightNow Technologies.

[8] Carr, David, "TD Bank's Social Strategy: Start Small, Think Big," *Informationweek*, January 19, 2012, http://www.informationweek.com/thebrainyard/news/social_networking_private_platforms/232500105/td-banks-social-strategy-start-small-think-big (accessed October 14, 2012).

[9] NCR Corp., "Most Shoppers Say Self-Checkout is Faster and a Service Differentiator, According to New Survey," http://www.ncr.com/newsroom/resources/most-shoppers-say-self-checkout-is-faster-and-a-service-differentiator-according-to-new-survey (accessed October 15, 2012).

[10] International Customer Management Institute, "ICMI 2010 Self-Service and the Multichannel Contact Center Report, " January 18, 2011, http://www.icmi.com/About-ICMI/Press-Room/2010-Self-Service-Research-Results (accessed October 15, 2012).

[11] Knowledge@Wharton, "Want to Improve Customer Service?"

[12] "18 Million Customers Flooding Social Networks To Speak To Brands," Fishburn-Hedges, June 2012, http://www.fishburn-hedges.co.uk/images/TheSMCustomerInfographic-FINALNEWTWITTERLOGO.pdf (accessed August 8, 2012).

[13] "Gartner Predicts That Refusing to Communicate by Social Media Will Be as Harmful to Companies as Ignoring Phone Calls or E-mails Is Today," Gartner, Inc. press release, August 1, 2012, http://www.gartner.com/it/page.jsp?id=2101515 (accessed August 8, 2012).

[14] Net Promoter Score is a simple but powerful assessment tool that divides customers into three categories: Promoters, Passives, and Detractors. Its fans include some of the world's largest companies. The Wikipedia description is at http://en.wikipedia.org/wiki/Net_Promoter.

[15] www.consumerwarningnetwork.com

Parting Shots

[1] Port25 is still alive and well at http://blogs.technet.com/b/port25.

[2] Legend has it that Federal Express founder Fred Smith got a C on a paper he wrote while an undergraduate at Yale that outlined the Federal Express business plan. The truth of that story is debated, however.